KT-473-035

Card Games

This is a Parragon Book
First published in 2001

Parragon
Queen Street House
4 Queen Street
Bath BA1 1HE, UK

Copyright © Parragon 2001

ISBN: 0-75255-189-2

All rights reserved. No part of this publication may be reproduced, stored in a retrieval system, or transmitted in any form or by any means, without the prior written permission of the copyright holder.

A copy of the CIP data for this book is available from the British Library upon request.

The right of Louis Canasta to be identified as the author of this work has been asserted in accordance with Section 77 of the Copyright, Designs and Patents Act of 1988.

Editorial, design and layout by Essential Books, 7 Stucley Place,
London NW1 8NS

Printed and bound in China

Card Games

Louis Canasta

p

Contents

Card Games For All the Family

The idea behind this book was to create a compendium of card games that would welcome in the curious and the beginners, yet not talk down to the seasoned card player who wants to learn new games. We knew we had to satisfy those who want a little wager, perhaps to while away a long journey, but the book had to be child-friendly and non-corrupting at the same time.

As a result, we've come up with a card game book that offers just a bit more than you might expect. *Pockets Card Games* teaches things you might not know about particular games – like how Rummy began life as a form of Poker in the Wild West saloons and why Piquet is an English game but all the terminology is in French. Such little bits of history are, we believe, highly appropriate, as people around the world have been playing cards since the medieval times – hence the somewhat archaic depictions on the court cards. And as so many games date back a hundred years or more, most of them arrive in this century with a story attached.

We wanted to offer choice too. There are over 100 different games and variations of games contained here, so there will always be something to suit the players, the time and the mood. Each has its own particular appeal, so if it's a contemplative, tactical session you're after, or a couple of hour's worth of rowdy knockabout fun, or something in between, you'll find it in here.

It's also a book that mixes the games up to such a degree that one involving farmyard impressions (Animals) sits alongside the game on which fortunes are won and lost (Baccarat). Which means there's always going to be something for everybody. Then to make sure there'll be a steady influx of new players and to make it easier for others to try out new games, we've included an at-a-glance box in each entry. These boxes outline how difficult or taxing the game is, how many players are needed and whether children will enjoy it too. The boxes also let you know how suitable each game is for gambling, if that is your pleasure. Then there's the detailed glossary which makes sense of the terms and jargon that crop up across a number of different games and can often baffle all but the expert card player.

This book aims to get the family sitting round the table again, playing cards and having fun. So what are you waiting for? Shuffle, cut, deal and enjoy yourselves.

suitability for children / gambling									
1	2	3	4	5	6	7	8	9	10
low				average					high

simplicity factor									
1	2	3	4	5	6	7	8	9	10
difficult				average					easy

skill factor									
1	2	3	4	5	6	7	8	9	10
low				average					high

guide to rating system

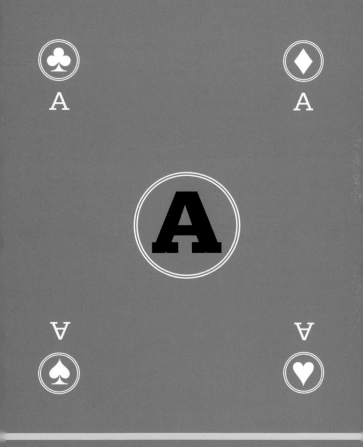

Aces Up

No. Players	One
Deck	Full
Score sheet	No
Aces	High
Origin	USA
Simplicity factor	10
Skill factor	2
Suitability for children	8

This game is also known as Idiot's Delight, but the name is a trifle unfair on a form of patience that is a fast-moving and fun, if unchallenging, distraction.

Four cards are dealt face-up next to each other and if a suit is represented more than once, the lower denomination card or cards are removed and placed on a discard pile. Four more cards are dealt on top of the others and into any spaces left by removed cards and the process is repeated. The game progresses as the removal of cards exposes cards that precipitate the removal of others. The next layer will only be dealt when there can be no further removal activity. Cards can be moved into empty spaces from the

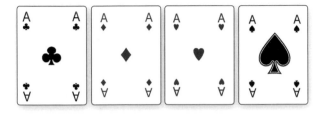

Aces up and we have a winner

top of other piles. The player will have won if he is left with four aces on the table and all other cards on the discard pile, he will have been beaten if there are any other cards left in the piles once the last set of four has been dealt.

Animals

No. Players	The more the merrier
Deck	Could be several
Score sheet	No
Origin	Germany
Simplicity factor	10
Skill factor	4
Suitability for children	10

An excellent, if rather noisy game for children, Animals can be highly entertaining for adults who've been in the pub all evening! In theory it can be played with two players, but the fun factor increases as the numbers go up. If the numbers get above half a dozen or so, multiple packs should be used.

Each player assumes the name of an animal of their choice, if necessary the packs are shuffled together and all the cards are dealt out face-down. In turn, each player turns over the top card of his pile to make a new face-up pile in front of them. This continues until two matching cards are turned over, at which point each player involved has to shout the other's animal name. The first

Animals

to do so captures the other player's face-up pile. When all a player's cards are gone, they drop out and the winner is the one who finishes up with all the cards.

Variations

It's always amusing for players to have to make a rival's animal noise instead of merely shouting the name.

Baccarat

No. Players	Any
Deck	Classic Baccarat uses three packs
Score sheet	No
Aces	Low
Origin	France
Simplicity factor	7
Skill factor	7
Suitability for children	7
Suitability for gambling	10

A casino-based, players-against-the-bank-type game that won't be much fun if you're not betting on it. Using three packs shuffled together, the banker deals two cards, face-down and individually, to each of the players, including himself as the last in the round. Players examine their cards then place their bets against the bank, who plays against each player separately.

Players have to add their cards up to a score of eight or nine, using a scoring system that has an ace valued as one, the pictures worth no points and the other cards scoring their number. If any of the players have a 'natural'

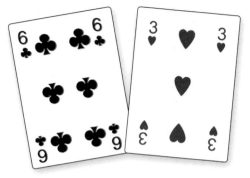

A natural nine

– a total of eight or nine from their original two cards –
and the dealer doesn't, they win and are paid out. If the
two cards add up to more than ten, only the last digit will
be used, for instance a hand of seven and nine would be
added together to make sixteen and would count as six.

If nobody has a natural, players will be dealt further
cards, face-up, and continue trying to make a total of
eight or nine without going over. Once they stop, the
dealer deals his own hand – with all cards face-up – to
try to get closer to eight or nine than he thinks his

opponents are, without going over the top.

Scoring

If a player and the banker both get cards adding up to eight or nine, nine wins out over eight. If a player gets the same score as the bank – either in a natural or otherwise – the bets are off.

Betting

The limit for wagers should be pre-set. If cards are dealt beyond the original two, then the stake can be increased before the turn of each new card.

Variations

Chemin-de-fer is the most popular variation of Baccarat, in which the dealer only plays against the player who has made the biggest bet, with the others having the choice to bet alongside that player or drop out.

Beat Your Neighbour

No. Players	Any
Deck	Full
Score sheet	No
Aces	High
Origin	USA
Simplicity factor	9
Skill factor	7 (if gambling)
Suitability for children	8
Suitability for gambling	9

In spite of its less-than-glamorous name, this game is actually quite a close relative of Stud Poker. But think how it would have sounded if, in the classic poker film *The Cincinatti Kid*, Steve McQueen had sat across the green baize with Edward G Robinson to play a game called Beat Your Neighbour!

Each of any number of players is dealt, singly, five cards that remain face-down in front of them. The first player turns over his top card, the player to his left turns over his cards until he beats the first player either with a higher card or a pair. As soon as he does this, he stops and the next player continues trying to beat what the

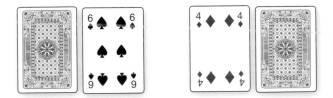

The top card wins

second one has, and so on. If a player turns all of his cards without beating the previous player, then he must drop out. Once everybody has had a turn, the first player continues to try to beat the last. This continues until only one player is left.

Betting

Players can bet up to a prescribed limit after each turn of their cards, wagering that their neighbour will not be able to beat them. The bets go into a pot that is collected by the winner.

Beggar My Neighbour

No. Players . .	Two upwards
Deck	Full, use two for six or more players
Score sheet	No
Aces	High
Origin	Great Britain
Simplicity factor	8
Skill factor	0
Suitability for children . . .	9

Though classically for two players only, there's no reason why Beggar My Neighbour can't involve as many as you like. All the cards are dealt out into face-down piles in front of each player. The first player turns up his top card into the middle of the table (the pot), the player on his left then does the same, and so on around the table until a player turns up a picture card or an ace. The player to his left must now turn up 'forfeit cards' on to the pot: one if the card turned up was a jack, two if it was a queen, three for a king, and four for an ace. If, during the forfeit, the player concerned turns up a picture card or an ace, the player to his left has to make the relevant forfeit. If the

Beggar my Neighbour

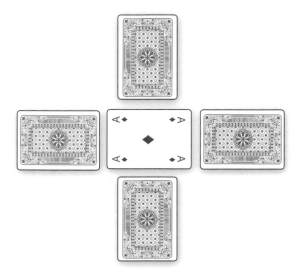

An ace forfeits four cards

forfeit is paid entirely in spot cards, the player who turned up the card that forced the forfeit picks up the pot and puts it, face-down, under his own pile.

When a player has run out of cards, he drops out. The winner is the player who ends up with all the cards.

Bezique

No. Players	Two
Deck .. Double piquet pack	
Score sheet	Yes
Aces	Low
Origin	France
Simplicity factor	1
Skill factor	9
Suitability for children ...	2
Suitability for gambling ..	6

The original sixteenth-century French version of what became Pinochle, Bezique is played by two players, with 64 cards. The game is in two parts and has a unique and rather complicated scoring system.

Two piquet packs (a piquet pack has a high ace and no cards below the seven) are shuffled together and eight cards dealt to each player – in the game's classical form these would be dealt as two threes then a two. The top card of the remainder determines trumps and is put on the bottom of the pile. If the non-dealer holds the seven in the trump suit, he can exchange it for the up card, and gains ten points. Whoever holds the other seven of

Bezique

trumps gains ten points when he plays it. The player other than the dealer leads. The dealer does not have to follow suit, but the only way to win the trick is either by playing a higher card of the suit that led or by trumping. If both players play the same card, the player that went first wins the trick.

The player who wins the trick adds it to his hand. He can then make melds (groups of cards of the same numerical value or same suit or in numerical sequence) with his hands and lay them down face-up on the table. One meld may be 'declared' and the score it earns added to that player's total. The trick's winner then takes the top card from the remaining pack, the trick's loser takes the next card. The trick's winner then replenishes his hand to bring the number of cards held back to eight.

The game continues with cards that have been laid down in melds remaining available for play. Cards may be re-used in subsequent declarations providing they are not the same type of meld as the card was originally used in. A jack of clubs that has already featured in a four-jack declaration can be re-declared in a king, queen, jack meld, but not another combination of four jacks. Once the pack has been exhausted, play goes on with opponents having to follow the lead suit if they can, until all tricks are played out.

Games can last for just that hand, or until one player amasses a prescribed number of points.

Scoring

- Melds are worth:
- Double bezique – 500
- Trump sequence – A, 10, J, Q, K of trumps – 250
- Any four aces – 100
- Any four kings – 80
- Any four queens – 60
- Any four jacks – 40
- Royal marriage (king and queen of trumps) – 40
- Bezique (queen and jack of any suit) – 40
- Plain marriage – king and queen of any suit other than trumps – 20
- Dix – when the up-card is exchanged for the seven of trumps – 10 (each)

At The End

- The winner of the final trick scores 10 points.
- Every 'brisque' – an ace or a 10 contained in a meld – scores the holder 10 points each.

A trump sequence

Penalties

- If a player draws out of turn his opponent scores 10.
- If a player's hand contains more than eight cards his opponent scores 100.

Betting

If playing one hand at a time, the difference in the two scores is translated into a pre-arranged fiscal value. If playing up to a points limit, the amount of the loser's shortfall would be converted into cash.

Variations

Three-Handed Bezique

The same as above, but played with three piquet packs (96 cards) and three players.

Rubicon Bezique

Played with four packs (128 cards) by two people who are dealt nine cards each. The first marriage declared determines trumps, games are one hand long and the scoring involves the following extra situations:

- Quadruple bezique – 4500
- Triple bezique – 1500
- A sequence (ace, 10, jack, queen, king) other than trumps – 150
- Carte Blanche – being dealt a first hand that contains no picture cards – 50
- Taking the final trick – 50 points
- Winning the game –500

Total scores are counted in 100s, being rounded down, so 1260 would become 1200. However, if the difference between winning and losing is less than 100 points, the winner will have won by 100. Brisques are only counted if the scores are tied, or added in if the loser is 'rubiconed', i.e. his total score is less than 1000. If this is the case, his score is added to the winner's, as is 320 for all the brisques that the winner holds and the win bonus is doubled to 1000. (In all variations of Bezique, it is only the loser that is rubiconed, even if both players fail to reach the prescribed score.)

Six-Pack Bezique

Sometimes called Chinese Bezique, this is played with six piquet decks (192 cards). Games are decided after one deal, players start with 12 cards, brisques never count and the following scores are added to Rubicon Bezique's system:

- Four trump aces – 1000
- Four trump kings – 800
- Four trump queens – 600
- Four trump jacks – 400
- Four trump tens – 900
- Carte Blanche – 250
- Taking the last trick – 250
- Winning the game – 1000
- The loser is rubiconed for a score of less than 3000.

Eight-Pack Bezique

Eight piquet packs (256 cards) are used and the players are dealt 15 cards each. The rules are the same as for Six-Pack Bezique with these additions to the score board:

- Quintuple Bezique – 9000
- Five trump aces – 2000
- Five trump kings – 1600
- Five trump queens – 1200
- Five trump jacks – 800
- Five trump tens – 1800
- The loser is rubiconed for a score of less than 5000.

Bouillotte

No. Players ..	Three to five
Deck	24 cards at most
Score sheet	No
Aces	High
Origin	France
Simplicity factor	9
Skill factor	9
Suitability for children ...	7
Suitability for gambling ..	8

This is the game that Poker is believed to have evolved from when it was taken to America by French settlers. It is played with three, four or five players.

For three players the pack is reduced to ace, king, 9, 8; for four, ace, king, queen, jack, 9, 8; and for five it is ace, king, queen, jack, 9, 8, 7. Each player is dealt three cards and the top card (the 'retourne') of the remainder is upturned in the centre of the table to be used by all players for scoring combinations. All players then compare hands, involving the retourne if necessary.

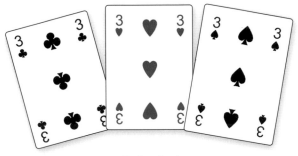

Brelan simple

Scoring

In descending order, the hands are ranked as follows: four of a kind using the retourne ('brelan carré'); three of a kind not using the retourne ('brelan simple') and three of a kind using the retourne ('brelan favori'). If nobody is holding a brelan, the player holding the highest card wins.

Betting

After players have looked at their hands, betting goes in rounds of raising stakes, much like Brag or Poker.

Brag

No. Players	Any
Deck	Full
Score sheet	No
Aces	High
Origin	England
Simplicity factor	10
Skill factor	3
Suitability for children	7
Suitability for gambling	8

The English forerunner of Poker, Brag never really made it in America, where it is often seen as 'Poker with the skill taken out'. Each player is dealt three cards and hands are compared to see whose can be arranged into the most valuable combination (see scoring). The highest hand wins. In classic English Brag there are three wild cards, Braggarts, the jack of clubs, the nine of diamonds and the ace of diamonds.

Scoring

Three aces is the highest hand, progressing down to three twos. Running flushes (cards of the same suit in sequential order), flushes (cards of the same suit) and runs (cards in sequential order, not of the same suit) using all three cards, are below three of a kind in that order and are ranked according to the highest card in each hand. (Some rules don't include these three combinations, but there's nothing wrong with them being used, provided all players have agreed to it beforehand.)

Pairs are below anything that uses all three cards. If two pairs are numerically the same, the player with the highest denomination spare card wins. There is no hierarchy among the four suits. In every case, a 'natural' hand beats a hand involving a braggart to achieve the same result.

If no player can make any combination, the hand containing the highest card is the winner.

Betting

Betting goes round the table from the left of the dealer, with each player seeing, raising or dropping out (see

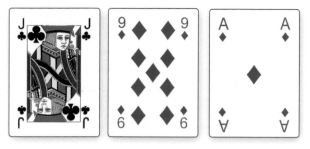

The three Braggarts

Poker), until those remaining agree to compare hands for the pot, exactly as in poker.

Variations

American Brag

Involves eight Braggarts – all the jacks and all the nines – and all Braggarts are of equal value, but a hand with a Braggart in it outranks the same naturally achieved hand. Thus three jacks is the highest score, followed by three nines.

Brag's highest hand

Five-Card Brag

Each player is dealt five cards, discarding two, face-down, to leave their best hand, before any betting or comparison starts.

Bridge

No. Players	Four
Deck	Full
Score sheet	Yes
Aces	High
Origin	Britain
Simplicity factor ..	Game 8
	Bidding 8
Skill factor	Game 5
	Bidding 8
Suitability for children ...	2
Suitability for gambling ..	6

A little over a hundred years old, Bridge evolved out of Whist. It is distinguished from that game by the bidding and scoring system, and the fact that it is played by four people who have been paired off. Explained as the main game here is Contract Bridge, by far the most popular version of the game, in which 'contracts' are 'bid' for by the partnerships, who then attempt to make the number of tricks they have declared they will. Bridge is a game of enormous subtlety and the best partnerships are those who have been playing together for a long time. There has been an entire library of books written on the game and how best to play it, what follows is merely the rules.

Bidding

All cards are dealt out to the four players and bidding takes place as soon as players have inspected their hands. In spite of them operating in tandem, there is supposed to be no communication between the partners once the game gets underway. Players are bidding for the contract, which is a declaration of how many tricks they believe their partnership can make. As they bid, they denote which suit will be trumps, or can bid 'no trumps' which means exactly that. Each contract declaration has its own ranking of value, depending on which suit, if any, is being called as trumps. As the bidding goes round the table, it escalates until all except one has 'passed' and the player who make the most valuable bid becomes the 'declarer'. Together with his partner, the declarer will then try to make the contract.

Each bid specifies how many tricks over the 'book'

(six tricks) partnerships believe they can make. In Bridge there is a hierarchy among the suits when they are called as trumps, with a 'no trumps' bid outranking them all. The bids in descending order are:

1) Seven no trumps (13 tricks, aka a grand slam, with all suits equal)

2) Seven spades (13 tricks with spades as trumps)

3) Seven hearts (13 tricks with hearts as trumps)

4) Seven diamonds (13 tricks with diamonds as trumps)

5) Seven clubs (13 tricks with clubs as trumps)

This will continue down to the lowest bid which is One clubs – seven tricks with clubs as trumps.

If players don't want to bid in a round of the auction they can say 'pass' and still bid in a later round, but if all four players pass on the first round, the cards are collected, shuffled and re-dealt. As well as passing or outbidding rivals, players can 'double' or 'redouble' opponents' calls. To double a bid means to assert that your partnership could prevent the bid being achieved if

Spades are the highest suit

it became a contract. If the players achieve this, the points scored by them will be doubled. If they fail to stop the contract being made, the declarer's points are doubled. If a potential declarer has had his bid doubled and the bidding comes back round to him without being raised, he can call 'redouble'. This means that should the bid become a contract, the scores are doubled from the double – quadruple what they would have originally been.

Playing

A full deck is dealt out and the declarer leads. As soon as he has played his first card his partner lays his hand face-upward on the table for the declarer to play that hand for him. This hand is called the 'dummy'. Tricks are played for as in Whist – won by the highest card played in the lead suit, or by trumping if there has been a trump suit designated. Tricks are collected in front of the declarer and one member of the other partnership. Once all 13 have been played the scores for that game are tallied up and entered on to the score sheet.

Scoring

Bridge score sheets are divided vertically and horizontally. The vertical line separates each partnership's scores and are usually headed 'We' and 'They' as it's advisable for both teams to keep a record of the scores. Each partnership can then score points that are recorded below and above the horizontal line.

Below the line points are for tricks won in completion of the contract once the book has been made, so they are for each trick made over six. Only the declaring partnership can win these trick points, and the values of the tricks depend on the suit called as trumps, and correspond to the hierarchy in the bidding process:

- Clubs and diamonds are worth 20 points per trick, 40 when doubled and 80 when redoubled
- Hearts and spades are worth 30 points per trick, 60 when doubled and 120 when redoubled
- No trumps are worth 40 points per trick, 80 when doubled and 160 when redoubled for the first trick and 30, 60 or 120 for subsequent tricks.

Bridge

we	they
150	180
70	
60	

A Bridge score sheet

Above the line are 'premium points'. The values change quite drastically once a partnership becomes 'vulnerable'. This occurs after a partnership has won one game towards a best-of-three rubber – both partnerships will be vulnerable once they've each won one game. The premium points are as follows:

Grand Slam or Small Slam

Completing a grand slam – 1000; if vulnerable – 1500

Completing a small slam (a bid of six, so 12 tricks have to be taken) – 500; if vulnerable – 750

Overtricks

For each trick taken over the number required by the contract:

Overtricks – the value of the trick

Doubled overtricks – 100; if vulnerable – 200 (regardless of the trick's value)

Re-doubled overtricks 200; if vulnerable – 400 (regardless of the trick's value)

Undertricks

These are added to opponent's score:

- First undertrick – 50; if vulnerable – 100
- Subsequent undertricks – 50; if vulnerable –100
- First doubled undertrick – 100; if vulnerable – 200
- Subsequent doubled undertricks – 200; if vulnerable – 300
- First redoubled undertrick – 200; if vulnerable – 400

- Subsequent redoubled undertricks – 400; if vulnerable – 600

Win Bonuses

- For making a doubled or redoubled contract – 50 (vulnerable or otherwise)
- For winning a three-game rubber 2-0 – 700
- For winning a three-game rubber 2-1 – 500
- For winning one game in an abandoned rubber – 300
- For having the only score in an abandoned game – 50

Honour Cards

Extra points are awarded before any cards are played for players holding what are known as honour cards in their original hands – this is for individual hands, not partnerships:

- A, K, Q, J, 10 of trumps – 150
- Any permutation of four from the above – 100
- Four aces (in a no trump game) – 150

A running score of the below-the-line points is kept, they

are added up after each hand and the first team to 100 trick points wins the game. When a partnership has won two games the rubber is decided by whichever has the higher total of trick and premium points when their scores from all of the games are added together.

Betting

A pre-agreed cash value for points is the best way, with amounts paid on the difference between the winning and losing totals.

Variations

Auction Bridge

An earlier game than Contract Bridge. Although the rules are the same, the scoring schedule is completely different. There is no vulnerability and all tricks made over the book are scored below the line, providing the declarer has made the contract – even if they are over the contract. Trick scores are:

Bridge

- Each trick won after book has been made – clubs – 6; diamonds – 7; hearts – 8; spades – 9
- Doubled – clubs –12; diamonds – 14; hearts – 16; spades – 18
- Redoubled – clubs – 24; diamonds – 28; hearts – 32; spades – 36

Other scoring disparites:

- Undertricks – scored by opponents, above the line
- Undoubled contract – 50 per trick; doubled – 100; redoubled – 200
- Grand slam – 100
- Small slam – 50

Each will be above the line.

Honour cards:

- A, K, Q, J, 10 of trumps in one hand – 100
- Four aces in one hand (no trumps) – 100
- A, K, Q, J, 10 of trumps split between partners 4-1 – 90
- Any four from above in one hand – 80
- A, K, Q, J, 10 of trumps split between partners 3-2 – 50

- Any four from above split between partners – 40
- Four aces split between partners – 40
- Three of the above-listed trumps in one hand – 30

The first partnership to score 30 points below the line wins the game, and the first to two games ends the rubber and scores a bonus 250 points. Above and below the line points are then totalled up as in Contract Bridge.

Three-handed Bridge

Four hands are dealt and one is left aside until after the bidding has finished – players bid as individuals rather than in pairs. The declarer then takes the extra hand, places it opposite himself and plays it as the dummy. Scoring is as for Contract Bridge. Each of the opponents is playing for his- or herself and, should the declarer fail to make the contract, they will each score the full number of above-the-line points. Likewise for honours and bonuses, and each player can be made vulnerable separately. Rubbers are played as the best of three, with a 2-0 score earning a bonus of 700 points and a 2-1 500.

Canasta

No. Players ..	Two pairs
Deck	Two
Score sheet	Yes
Origin ..	South America
Simplicity factor	3
Skill factor	7
Suitability for children	2
Suitability for gambling	8

Essentially a variation of Rummy, Canasta is played with two packs, all the jokers and two pairs of players seated opposite each other. Suits are irrelevant in Canasta, as cards are matched by denomination only.

Eleven cards are dealt to each player. The remaining deck is put in the middle of the table, face-down with the top card upturned and placed next to the pile to start a face-up discard stack, known as 'the pot'. In turn, players take the top card from the face-down stack, absorb it into their hand and discard one on to the pot. Players are attempting to make 'melds' by laying sets of three or more cards of the same denomination face-up in front of them.

Canasta

Points are scored in running team totals for each card laid down. New cards can be added to a players or his partner's melds (but not their opponents') at any stage during the game. The hand is won as soon as a player gets rid of all of his cards. However, a player cannot put down all his cards until he and his partner have made a 'canasta' by melding seven of the same denomination cards. Jokers and deuces can be used as wild cards to make the canasta but there are the following limit to the number of wild cards used in a meld: one in a three-card meld, two in a four-card meld and three in five or over (including a canasta).

At any time, players may pick up the entire pot instead of a card from the face-down pile. While these extra cards may be necessary for them to make canasta, it can also give them many other cards to have to meld. (In some variations of canasta, the pot cannot be taken up unless that player's team has already made a meld of

50 points or more, or can use the top card on the pot as part of a meld that doesn't involve a wild card.)

Games are usually won by the first pair to make 5,000 points.

Scoring

Canasta's scoring system is what makes essentially a simple game suddenly very complicated. Scores are awarded to the players for the cards they've laid down in melds and added to the score sheet as the melds are made.

The wild cards – jokers and deuces – regardless of what they are used to represent, are worth 50 and 20 points respectively; king, queen, jack, ten, nine and eight all score ten each; seven, six, five and four all score five.

Threes are special: red threes are placed face-up as soon as a player gets one, a replacement card is drawn and each scores 100 points. If a player is dealt all four red threes and places them down together the bonus is 800. Black threes cannot be melded except by a player

Canasta

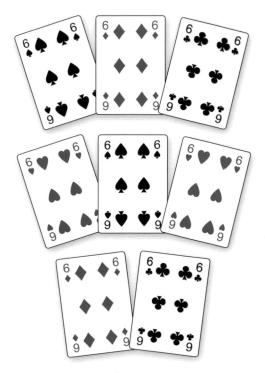

A canasta

going out, they only count for five points and should be discarded immediately.

Canastas score bonus points as well as the cards' total: a 'natural canasta' (no wild cards) earns 500 bonus points, a 'mixed canasta' (involving wild cards) scores 300. A hundred points are awarded to the team that wins, while that can be doubled if a player goes out 'concealed' by melding his entire 11 cards without making any previous melds. After a team has won, the points value of the losers' unmelded cards is totalled up and subtracted from their existing score.

Betting

Points for cash – a prearranged value – with the difference between the two team scores at the end constituting the 'pot'.

Variations

In Two-handed Canasta each player has 15 cards and must make two canastas before going out. Three-

Canasta

handed Canasta is played with 13 cards and two canastas. Six-handed Canasta involves three packs, two teams of three seated opposite each other, two canastas to end a hand and is played up to 10,000 points, with a meld of five red threes being worth 1,000 points and all six 1,200. Cutthroat Canasta is a variation of Three-handed Canasta in which if a player takes the pot, the other two immediately become a team against him.

Casino

No. Players	Two to four
Deck	Full
Score sheet	Yes
Aces	Low in playing, hig scoring
Origin	France
Simplicity factor	4
Skill factor	8
Suitability for children	7
Suitability for gambling	6

To play this medieval French game, it helps if you're good at maths, as it's all about finding as many combinations of numbers as quickly as you can. Sometimes spelled Cassino, it can be played with two, three or four players and used to be very popular in casinos with players playing against the bank.

Four cards are dealt, face-down and in pairs, to each player. After the dealer has dealt to himself, four cards are dealt, again in pairs, in a face-up row in the middle of the table. These extra cards are known as the 'layout'. The player to the dealer's left then tries to 'capture' as many cards as possible from the layout by matching them, numerically, with cards in his hand. He does this by placing the card from his hand, face-down, on top of the card it matches. For instance, if the player holds the eight of clubs and the eight of hearts is showing in the layout, the player puts his eight of clubs face-down on the eight of hearts, removes it from the layout and places this trick in front of him.

The player can also capture tricks if a combination of cards showing in the layout numerically equals a card in his hand. For example, if the five of spades, the ace of clubs and the two of diamonds were in the layout they would add up to eight (aces count as one) and so could be 'captured' by an eight to make a trick.

More than one capture can also be performed in tandem. For example, if the layout comprised the eight of hearts, five of spades, ace of clubs and two of diamonds, the eight of clubs could be used to make both captures simultaneously. In this case, all four layout cards would be gathered together and the eight of clubs placed face-down on top to form one fat trick. To take all four cards in one capture is called a 'sweep'. Court cards can only be captured as pairs or when three of one denomination are in the layout and the player making the capture holds the fourth.

When tricks are gathered in, it's important the card that made the capture remains face-down with the others face-up, as in the scoring system only captured cards score points. Also, any sweeps made must be identifiable at the end.

As an alternative to straight captures, players can make 'builds'. Building involves laying cards from their hands face-up on layout cards, to make a total that adds up to a card in their hand, with the intention of capturing it next time around. For example, if the layout shows the three of hearts and the player hold the five of clubs and the eight of spades, he would put his five face-up on the table next to the three, announce that he was 'building eight' and capture it with his eight on his next

The eight can capture the three and five build

turn. However, his build is open to attack from other players who, if they can, may build on top of it. If the next player had a two and a ten in his hand, he could put the two down, face-up, next to the five, announce he was 'building ten' and wait for it to come around to make the capture. But if the next player along also had a ten then that capture could be his. The more players involved in a game, the riskier building becomes.

Player can create 'multiple builds' by building on two layout cards or existing builds with the aim of capturing them both with the same card held in their hand. If a player holds an eight, a two, a four and a king and the layout shows a four and a build that totals six, he can announce 'building eights' (note the plural). He will then, move his two targets next to each other, build the four on the other four and his two on the build of six and wait for his next turn to capture both tricks. Tripartite multiple builds are also possible. Although each aspect of multiple builds can continue to be built on, once announced the value cannot be changed.

Casino

Once a player has started a build, on his next turn he must capture that build, add to another one or start a new one. If he can't then he adds one of the cards from his hand face-up as part of the layout. As soon as all the players have played all the cards in their hand, they are dealt another four (once again in pairs) but no more cards are added to the layout. Each new deal is called a 'round' and a game will last for six rounds. When all the players have played all their cards on the sixth round, the player who made the most recent capture picks up the remaining layout cards and the score are counted. The player with the most points wins the game.

Scoring

Only captured cards score points.
- If a player has captured more than 26 cards (half the pack) they score 3
- Seven captured spades (of any denomination) – 1
- Each sweep made – 1
- Each ace captured – 1

- 10 of diamonds (known as 'Big Casino') – 2
- Ace of spades ('Little Casino') – 1

Variations

Draw Casino

Instead of waiting for each player to play out their four cards before everybody is dealt new cards, players replenish their hands by drawing from the pot as they go along, and the game is played until the pot is exhausted.

Spade Casino

In this version, the ace, jack and two of spades are worth two points each; every other captured spade is worth one point.

Casino Royale

The court cards have a value – kings 13, queens 12 and jacks 11 – allowing them to be captured and used as part of builds.

Clock Patience

No. Players	One
Deck	Full
Score sheet	No
Aces	Low
Simplicity factor	10
Skill factor	0
Suitability for children	8

A simple, fast-moving and entertaining form of patience, ideal for children as there's about a fifty per cent chance of winning. Thirteen face-down stacks of four cards are dealt out with twelve arranged in a circle like the numbers on a clock and the remaining stack put to one side of the 'face'. Of this stack, the top card is turned up and placed on the stack in the position of its number on the clock face. For example, a six would be put at the bottom of the circle, where the six is on a clock. The ace represents one o'clock, the jack eleven o'clock and queen is midday.

When a card is placed on a stack, the bottom card from that stack is taken out, turned over and then put in its correct place from where the bottom card is taken

and moved on to its correct place, and so on. If a king is turned up it will be put into a row in the centre of the 'clock' and the next card will be taken from the pile that has been put aside. The idea is to turn all the cards in the clock face over before the fourth king is turned up and there are no more reserve cards to draw upon.

Concentration

No. Players .... Any	
Deck .... full	
Score sheet .... No	
Simplicity factor 7	
Skill factor 8	
Suitability for children ... 10	

A long way from the likes of Stud Poker or Contract Bridge, this is a traditional parlour game that loses nothing by being played with playing cards instead of a 'purpose built' concentration pack.

A whole pack (including jokers, if you like) is dealt out face-down on a table so they are not covering up or touching each other. (You'll need a pretty big table!) The first player turns over any one card so everybody can see it, then puts it back face-down in the same place and repeats the process with another. The other players, in turn, do the same. The aim is to pick pairs matched by value and colour – the red jacks, the black fives and so on – which are then taken out of the game and placed in front of the player who picked them. This player then has another turn and continues until he fails to match two cards. Where the concentration comes in is in remembering cards' positions in order to make the matches. The winner is the player who finishes the game with the most pairs in front of them.

Cribbage

No. Players	Two to four
Deck	full
Score sheet	If not using a board
Ace	Low
Origin	Great Britain
Simplicity factor	3
Skill factor	8
Suitability for children	6
Suitability for gambling	7

Dating back to 17th century, Cribbage requires an agile, numerate mind and really ought to be played with a Crib Board (see scoring) to mark the scores as the game progresses. It can be scored with pencil and paper, but the true way to win at cribbage is to be the first to go 'twice round the board', scoring 121 points. Essentially a two-handed game, it can be played with three or four but rarely is.

Each player is singly dealt six cards. After inspecting their hand, they each discard two cards that become the 'crib'. The player who didn't deal cuts the remaining pack and the dealer turns over the top card of the lower

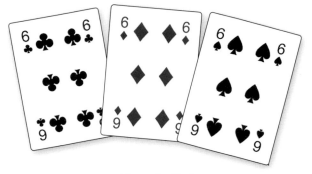

Three of a kind

half to become the 'starter'. (This will not be used in the game, but may come into account during the scoring.)

The non-dealer then plays a card from his hand face-up on the table on his side of the board and calls out its value. The dealer does the same on his side and announces the total value of the two cards. If the first card played was a five, and the second a three, the dealer would call 'eight'. This goes on until the total amounts to nearly 31, the figure it must not exceed. If the cards in a player's hand will 'bust' 31 if played, he calls 'Go'. The other player must either play a card that will keep it below 31, or make it exactly 31 or call 'Go' himself. After that, the cards played are turned face-down, moved to one side and play resumes. If only one player is left holding cards, then he plays them out by himself.

Cards are worth their face value, with court cards counting as ten during the sequence building, and scoring (see below) takes place as this goes on.

After all the cards have been played comes the 'show', in which first the non-dealer then the dealer count up the combinations they can make with cards they have played – both can involve the starter in making as many permutations as possible. The dealer then does the same with the crib (again the starter is included) and adds those scores to his own. Following the show, if neither score is at 121 then another six-card hand is dealt, with the non-dealer of the previous round becoming the dealer, and the game continues until one player has been round the board twice.

Scoring

There are two scoring schedules in cribbage, one for points earned during play and one applied to the show.

During Play

These are points scored for combinations of cards as they are laid on the table. They will involve both players' cards – if one puts down a four of clubs to call 'four', then the other plays the four of hearts he will call 'eight for a pair' and score two points for the pair. If the first player than plays the four of spades he will call 'twelve for three' and score six points for a 'royal pair', that is three cards of the same rank which can be made into three different pairs (4H+4S; 4H+4C; 4S+4C).

Ideally, these points would be racked up on the cribbage board (see below). If not a running total must be kept on a score sheet. The schedule of combinations is as follows:

• Pair (two cards of same rank) – 2
• Royal Pair (three cards of same rank) – 6

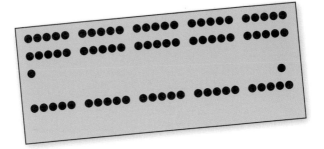

Twice round the board wins the game

- Double Royal Pair (four cards of same rank) – 12
- Run (numerical sequence of more than three cards of any suit, not necessarily played in order, so 5H, 3C, 4H, 6D would count) – 3 points for making the first three, then one point per card after that.
- Flush (cards of any numerical order, but in the same suit) – 4 for making the first four, then 1 per card after that.
- Running Flush (in numerical order and the same suit) – points are scored for both run and the flush.

- Fifteen (the sequence totalling exactly fifteen) – 2
- If the starter card is a jack, the dealer scores 2 'for his heels'.

The Show

The show is scored in exactly the same way as during play – pairs, runs, flushes and total of fifteen – with first the non-dealer then the dealer making as many combinations as they can from their own hand. All of their cards can be used in as many different combinations as possible, and each player will include the starter as if it were a card they'd been dealt.

If either player's hand includes the jack of the same suit as the starter, they score an extra point. This is called 'One for his nob'.

The Crib

After the dealer has totalled his own show, he will do the same with the four cards that make up the crib, once again involving the start, and adds the score to his own.

Penalties

If a player calls 'Go' but could actually have played a card, the cards he is left holding will be removed from play and his opponent scores two points.

If a player fails to play his cards after his opponent has called 'Go', the same penalty applies.

If a player gets round the board twice before his opponent has got round once, it's called a 'lurch' and the winner pegs two games.

A Cribbage Board

This is a wooden board with a series of holes divided into two rows of six sets of five. Each player takes a side, moving two pegs up one row and down the other (going round the board). Tally is kept by the pegs being leapfrogged as the totals mount, so if a player scores three points he moves his first peg up three places; then if his next score is two, he'll place the second peg two holes on from that, and so on.

Two extra rows of ten holes in the centre are used to

keep track of games won by each player, with a rubber usually lasting until one player has pegged all ten of these holes.

Variations

Five- or Seven-Handed Cribbage

Cribbage can be played with five cards or seven cards. In each case the crib is still made up from two cards from each hand and the rules are exactly the same as for the six-card game. In Five-Handed Cribbage the non-dealer pegs three points for not having the crib. In Seven-Handed Cribbage games are played to three times round the board or 181 points.

Three-Handed Cribbage

Players are dealt five cards and put one each into the crib, which is then dealt one more to bring it up to four. The sequences run round the table with players calling 'Go' to the player on their left. Otherwise, the rules are as for the conventional game.

Partnership Cribbage

This involves four players in pairs sitting opposite each other. They are dealt five cards each and put one each in the crib. Sequences run round the table, as does the calling of 'Go'. Points made during play are individual but pegged along the same row on the board and partners' cards are pooled for the show.

Donkey

No. Players	Up to 13
Deck . . . . varies according . . . . to the number of players	
Score sheet	Yes
Simplicity factor	10
Skill factor	7
Suitability for children . . .	10

A children's game that can be of enormous amusement value for adults, especially after a few drinks!

Up to 13 players can play and the pack will be adjusted accordingly, with one set of four same-value cards being used per player. These can be any sets, as the game concerns their similarity not their face value. Each player is dealt four cards. Simultaneously, each player passes a card of his choice to the player on his left. The process repeated until a player has four cards the same. When they do, they lay their hand down and make a pre-arranged signal, which can be as silly as you like – braying like a donkey is a favourite, or standing on your chair. On this sign, the other players must do the same thing and the last to do so loses, making them the donkey.

Ecartre

No. Players .... Two	
Deck ...... No cards below a seven	
Aces .... High	
Origin .... France	
Simplicity factor 5	
Skill factor 7	
Suitability for children 4	
Suitability for gambling ... 5	

Ecartre is a game that used to be very popular in French casinos, where it always attracted a good deal of side-betting and had a very complicated scoring system of penalties and bonuses. The game described here is the domestic version, which is much more straightforward. That said, the scoring system still seems disproportionate to the actual play.

Using a piquet pack (no cards higher than a seven), two players are dealt five cards each with the next card turned up to determine trumps. If the non-dealer decides he can win three tricks he announces he will play and the game commences, playing for tricks by going higher in

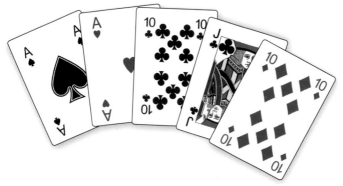

A hand worth proposing

the same suit or trumping. If he doesn't think he can make three tricks, he will 'propose' and if it is 'accepted' by the dealer, he can discard any number of cards from his hand and be dealt new ones. The dealer can then do the same. If the dealer opts not to accept the proposal, the game is played without exchanging any cards. Each hand continues until all five tricks are won, points are cumulative from hand to hand, and the deal changes after each hand.

Scoring

- If the card turned up for trumps is a king, the dealer scores 1.
- If either player wins three or four tricks they score 1.
- Taking all five tricks is called a vole and earns 2.
- If either player has made three or four tricks when there was no proposal, or the proposal was refused, he wins an extra point. (In each of these cases, it's still only two points for making all five.)
- The winner is the first player to five points.

Betting

Away from the obvious attractions of side-betting, it's best just to settle up at the end of each game with the difference between the players' scores determining what is paid out.

Eights

No. Players	Two to six
Deck	Full
Score sheet	Yes
Aces	Low
Origin	Germany
Simplicity factor	8
Skill factor	7
Suitability for children	9
Suitability for gambling	6

A fast-moving game that is sometimes known as Stops, Eights and can be played with two to six players.

If the game is for two, three or four players, seven cards are dealt to each, if five or six players, five cards.

The top card of the remainder is turned up and placed next to it. The player to start has to cover this with a card of the same value or same suit from his hand. If he can't, he draws cards from the pot (the pile of remaining cards) until he can, and the game continues. All four eights are 'wild' and can be played at any time and nominated as any suit, which then has to be followed by the next player in turn. For example, the eight of hearts could be played on top of the queen of spades, and clubs be declared, so the next player has to follow with a club.

The winner is the first player to get rid of all his cards, and scores points from the others relative to the value of the cards they are still holding. If play is stopped as no player can go, the values of each player's hand is counted and the winner is the one with the lowest score.

Scoring

When the players' hands have to be counted, each eight scores 50 points, picture cards 10 each and the others score their face value with an ace counting as one.

Betting

A simple points-for-cash system is advised, with the losing players each paying the winner the value of their hands.

Euchre

No. Players	Two to four
Deck	No cards lower than seven
Score sheet	Yes
Aces	High
Origin	France
Simplicity factor	8
Skill factor	6
Suitability for children	3
Suitability for gambling ...	5

A quick and straight-to-the-point game, Euchre was once the most popular trumps game in the USA, although its origins are French. Speedy as the actual game is, however, there are certain conventions that have to be established before play can begin. Euchre can be played with two, three or four players, but, as it is the most straightforward, the two-player game is explained here.

The pack features no cards lower than a seven and aces are high unless in the trump suit. In that case, the highest value card is the jack of trumps (known as 'the right bower') with the jack of the same colour ('the left bower') being the second highest in the pack, then the trump suit runs down as normal – ace, king, queen, ten, nine and so on.

Each player is dealt five cards, as a three and a two, then the next card of the remainder is turned face-up to signify trumps. If the non-dealer reckons he can make at least three tricks with that suit as trumps, but with the dealer having that particular trump (the turned-up card) in his hand, he announces 'I'll take it up', and the dealer discards a card to take up the turned-up card. If he doesn't believe he can make that many tricks with that suit as trumps he says 'I'll pass'. The dealer then gets the chance to 'bid', which he does in exactly the same way, taking up the upturned card if he accepts that suit as trumps. When the dealer decides to take it up or pass, he is doing so in the knowledge that the upturned card will be part of his hand.

If both players pass on this first round of bidding, the non-dealer can nominate any suit he likes as trumps if he thinks he can thus take at least three tricks. If he passes,

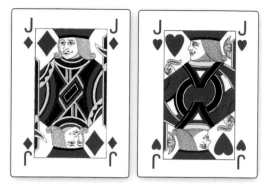

A right bower and a left bower

the dealer has the same opportunity. If they both pass, the hands are folded and the cards are dealt again.

The object is to take as many tricks as possible in the conventional manner – the non-dealer or the winner of the last trick leads, the highest card in that suit or trump (with the right and left bowers being the highest cards) takes the trick. The object is to take as many tricks as possible. Scoring takes place at the end of each hand.

Games are played to the first player reaching a pre-agreed total (usually seven, nine or ten) from a series of hands or the most points after a set number of games.

Scoring

Each trick won – 1

- Either player taking three or four tricks – 1
- The player who called trumps not taking three tricks (he is 'euchred') – 2 points subtracted
- Either player taking five tricks (a 'march') – 2

Betting

A cash-for-points system, paid on the differences between the scores at the end of the game, is the obvious method.

Variations

Cutthroat Euchre

The rules are the same for this three-handed version as for the two-handed game, so the player who calls trumps has to make his march against two other players. Three points are awarded for a march, but when a player is euchred both his opponents gain two points.

Four-Handed Euchre

Four players play as two partnerships sitting opposite each other. The rules are the same, but, during the bidding process, if the dealer's partner wants to let the dealer know he wants the suit of the face-up card as trumps he announces 'I assist', and the dealer will know to take it up. The other partnership has no such privileges, and their taking up those trumps will still put the face-up card into the dealer's hand. Although players play individually, their scores are totalled up as a partnership, and the scoring is as for the two-handed game. However, the player who bids trumps can declare they are 'going it alone', at which point their partner folds his hand and the game continues as for three-handed euchre.

Auction Euchre

This is played by two partnerships, but without the turned-up trump. Each player bids for how many tricks they think they could make – three, four or five – with their as yet undeclared choice of trumps. The highest bid wins the right to chose trumps and if the bidding team makes that number of tricks, they score that many points. If they are euchred, the other team scores the amount bid.

Fan Tan

No. Players	Three to eight
Deck	Full
Score sheet	No
Aces	Low
Simplicity factor	9
Skill factor	5
Suitability for children	8
Suitability for gambling	10

Played with three to eight players, Fan Tan is a cousin of Eights but is less complicated and far more suitable for gambling.

All the cards are dealt and the player to the dealer's left has to play any seven. If he hasn't got one he puts a chip into the pot and the player to his left has to play one. If he can't the same thing happens, but if he can, the player to his left has to follow suit with either the six or the eight and the next player has to follow with, depending on what was played, the five or the nine. This goes up or down to the king or the ace respectively, with any player who can't follow putting a chip into the pot before the next player tries. Once a suit has run out, another seven has to be

Fan Tan

A typical Fan Tan sequence

played and the process is repeated. The winner is the player who gets rid off all his cards first. He takes the pot and one chip for every card in the hands of each of the other players.

Five Hundred

No. Players	Two to five
Deck	seven upwards plus one joker
Score sheet	Yes
Aces	High
Origin	USA
Simplicity factor	9
Skill factor	7
Suitability for children	3
Suitability for gambling	6

Very similar to Euchre, with elements of Pinochle, this 100-year-old game is essentially a three-hander, but has variations that can involve up to five players. It is one of the very few card games in which spades is not the highest-ranked suit.

It is played with a 33-card pack that features nothing lower than a seven, but with the addition of a joker. The joker becomes the most valuable card in whichever suit is trumps (it is known as the 'best bower'), followed by, as in Euchre, the jack of trumps (the 'right bower') and then the jack of the same colour (the 'left bower').

Ten cards are dealt to each player, in two parcels of

Five Hundred

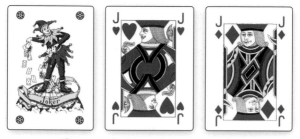

The most valuable cards in Five Hundred

three and one of four. A 'widow' parcel of three is put aside between the first and second round of dealing.

Auction-style bidding then begins as the three players declare how many tricks they think they can take with whatever suit they call as trumps, or without trumps. As the auction progresses upward, each bid is called a 'jump'. Players can pass if they want to and if all three pass, the hand is void, the deals passes to the left and the cards are shuffled and re-dealt. There is a progressive value of bids (see the following table) running from six tricks with spades as trumps (40) to ten tricks with no trumps (520). The highest bidder takes up the unseen widow cards, and discards any three cards he chooses. He then leads for the first trick.

Tricks are played for as normal and, although the contract winner is now effectively playing against the other two players, they will both count their scores separately.

Scores are kept cumulatively from hand to hand and the winner is the first to 500. Hence the name. If more than one player reaches 500 in the same hand, then whoever won that contract takes preference, or if there is no contract winner involved it's the player who got there first.

Scoring

If the contract winner makes his contract he scores the number of points it is worth (see the following box). If he doesn't the same amount will be deducted from his total, which could result in a minus figure.

Each of the two non-contract winners scores 10

points for each trick they take. If the contract is for less than nine tricks but the contract winner makes all ten, then he scores 250 points on top of the value of the contract.

Trumps	6 Tricks	7 Tricks	8 Tricks	9 Tricks	10 Tricks
Spades	40	140	240	340	440
Clubs	60	160	260	360	460
Diamonds	80	180	280	380	480
Hearts	100	200	300	400	500
No Trumps	120	220	320	420	520

Variations

Two-Handed Five Hundred

Played to the same rules, with the same number of cards. Three hands are dealt but the third one is left face-down while the two players play out the hand.

Four-Handed Five Hundred

Two pairs compete against each other and score together. The pack includes the sixes, fives and red fours. Apart from that, the rules are essentially the same.

Five-Handed Five Hundred

A full pack including the joker is used to make 53 (five hands of ten and a three-card widow). The successful contract bidder can chose a partner by nominating a specific card and whoever has it has to play with him against the other three.

Giveaway

No. Players	Two to six
Deck	Full
Score sheet	No
Aces	Low
Origin	Britain
Simplicity factor	7
Skill factor	8
Suitability for children	8
Suitability for gambling	0

This is a game that requires a degree of quick wit to make up for the luck involved in the fact that players cannot see their own cards until they play them.

Giveaway can be played with up to six players. All cards are dealt out into face-down piles in front of the players. It doesn't really matter if they have slightly unequal amounts. The first player turns over his top card and if it is any of the four aces he puts it in the middle of the table and turns over another, which, if it's the two of the same suit as the ace, he puts it on top of the ace. If his first card isn't an ace, it is placed face-up in front of him. The next player then turns up his top card.

Giveaway

If it is the next card in suit and sequence to that on centre pile or the previous player's pile, he can add it to that pile and play again. If he can't add a card to any piles, he places the card in front of him and play continues round the table.

The idea is to make sequences on any upturned card on the table. If a player has turned up a nine of clubs and any other player has either the ten or the eight showing he can add his card to their pile. Any player who can follow a sequence carries on turning cards until they can't, when the card is put on their own face-up pile.

When a player has played through all of the cards in his hand he inverts his face-up pile and carries on playing. The winner is the first to get rid of all his cards on to either the centre piles or other players' piles.

Go Boom!

No. Players	Two to six
Deck	Full
Score sheet	No (unless the game is being scored)
Aces	High
Origin	USA
Simplicity factor	9
Skill factor	3
Suitability for children ...	10

A very simple game for between two and six players, Go Boom! is particularly suitable for young children as a step up from Snap!

Seven cards are dealt to each player and the remainder makes up a face-down pot. The player to the left of the dealer leads. The other players must match that card either by face value or suit. For example, the queen of hearts could be followed by any heart card or any other queen. The winner of the trick is whoever played the highest card in the suit that was led.

If any player can't follow either suit or value they must draw cards from the pot, until they can either follow suit or value or have taken three cards. The winner is the first player to get rid of all the cards in their hand. The only advantage of winning tricks is that the winner leads for the next trick, otherwise they don't count for anything. The winner will announce his victory by shouting 'Boom!' as he plays his last card.

Scoring

As a rule, games of Go Boom! are not scored as that tends to slow the pace down, but there is a system which can be put in place. Once a game has been won, the cards each player is left holding are totted up and added to a running total on a score sheet. Aces count for 11, picture cards 10, and everything else at face value. Once one player has reached a prearranged score, the game ends and the overall winner is whoever has the lowest score.

Variations

Crazy Eights

This involves exactly the same rules as above, but the four eights in the pack can count as any card, therefore will win whatever trick they are played on. If more than one eight is played in the same trick, the one in the led suit takes priority, if there is one, otherwise the ranking is spades, hearts, diamonds and lastly clubs. If scoring Crazy Eights, any eight left in a player's hand incur 50 points.

Go Fish

No. Players	Two to five
Deck	Full
Score sheet	No
Origin	USA
Simplicity factor	8
Skill factor	6
Suitability for children	10

This is an entertaining American game for two to five players that relies on cunning and memory as much as traditional card game skills. Five cards are dealt per player if there are four or five players and seven if there are two or three. The remainder is put face-down in the centre as a pot.

The idea is to make 'books' – sets of four cards of a similar value – by asking fellow players for particular cards. To start, the player to the left of the dealer can ask any other player in the game for particular cards, saying 'give me your sevens' (or whatever). The player asked must hand them over if he has them and the player who asked has another go. If he hasn't he tells him to 'Go Fish!' and the player who asked must take the top card

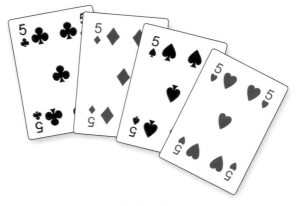

A 'book' of fives

off the pot. If this is of the value he demanded or is the final card needed to make any book (not just of the value he was asking for) he can take another turn and once again ask any player for any cards. If not, he places the card in his hand and the player on his left takes a turn.

Books made are placed down on the table and the winner is the first player to have put all his cards down in books, which ends the game.

Good Morning Jack

No. Players	Any
Deck	Several
Origin	USA
Simplicity factor	9
Skill factor	3
Suitability for children	10

Good Morning Jack has such an enormous potential for downright silliness that, while it is essentially a fast-moving game that can give children a great deal of fun, it also has an almost unlimited post-pub appeal.

There can be any number of players, but if it gets to be more than about five, it's best to use more than one deck of cards shuffled together. All the cards are dealt out face-down in front of each player. The first player leads by turning his top card up in the middle of the table, the next player does the same, putting his on top of the first and so on around the table. There are a number of 'score cards'. When they are turned up, every player must perform a prescribed action and the last to do so takes the pile in the middle and adds it, face-down, to the bottom of his pile. If a king is turned up the players must salute the king – literally. If it's a queen they must bow to the queen. They have to say 'Good Morning Jack' to a jack and knock on the table for a seven.

The fun starts as the pace gets quicker and the players more careless and carelessly anticipatory. To spice things up, other actions can be added for any of the other cards – stand up for the two; pull your left ear for the five; stand up and turn around for the ten and so on. The winner is the first player to get rid of all his cards, but on playing his last one he must say 'Last card'. If he doesn't, he takes the pot and the game continues.

Hearts

No. Players	Three to eight
Deck	Full
Score sheet	No
Aces	High
Origin	France
Simplicity factor	8
Skill factor	8
Suitability for children	7
Suitability for gambling	7

A straightforward, enjoyable game that has been spiced up over the centuries with a number of different variations, Hearts can be played with between three and eight players.

In its simplest form, all the cards are dealt out face-down – to keep the hands equal up to four low denomination cards (other than hearts) will be removed – and each player looks at his hand. There are no trumps, so tricks are won by the highest card of the lead suit, and only players unable to follow suit can discard. Tricks are amassed in front of the players who won them and the winner leads the next trick. When all are played, the cards are turned face-up and each player scores one

Don't take tricks with hearts in them

point for every heart card in his haul. Scores are totalled, hand by hand, and games finish as soon as a player has 50 points, with the winner being the one with the lowest total. The idea is therefore not to take tricks with hearts in them.

If agreed in advance, after looking at their hand each player can pass four cards to the player on their left.

Betting

On a hand-by-hand basis, every player puts in a

The Black Maria

prescribed amount for each heart he's left holding and the winner takes the pot. If being scored cumulatively, an average of the players' totals is taken and those above it put the amount they are over it in the pot while those below it take out the amount they are below it.

Variations

Black Maria

The most common variation, in which the player who

ends up with the queen of spades scores an extra 13 points, but the player finishing up with the jack of diamonds deducts 10 points from his score.

Black Widow

The same as Black Maria, except that the full 52 cards are used regardless of how many players. Any cards left over after the deal – the widow – are given to the winner of the first trick, who is the only player permitted to look at them, to be counted in his score for that hand.

Pink Lady

As Black Maria, but with the queen of hearts also counting for 13 points.

Take All Hearts

In this version, if any player, in any of the above variations, takes all the hearts and any other penalty or bonus cards, score is deducted instead of added to his total.

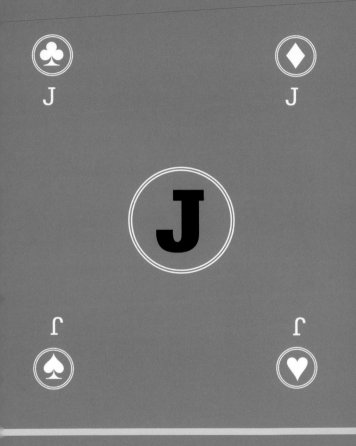

Jacks

No. Players	Three
Deck	Full
Score sheet	No
Aces	High
Origin	France
Simplicity factor	9
Skill factor	7
Suitability for children	7
Suitability for gambling	5

Sometimes called Knaves, this game is not dissimilar to Whist but it is played with just three players and has a different cumulative scoring system.

The whole of a full deck is dealt out to the three players, with the remaining card turned over to establish trumps. The thirteen tricks are competed for as in Whist – the highest in the led suit or a trump wins – and players collect the tricks they've won in front of them. Once a hand is complete, players count their scores as one point for each trick won, but tricks containing each of the four jacks incur penalty points so hands can end up with minus scores. The idea is therefore to take as many tricks

Avoid the jacks

as possible, but to avoid the ones with jacks in them. Games are usually stopped when a player has reached 20 points.

Scoring

One point is gained for each trick won, but the following points are deducted from players' totals if they finish up with tricks with jacks in them: jack of spades – one point; jack of clubs – two; jack of diamonds – three; jack of hearts – four.

Betting

Having prearranged a cash-for-points value, the two losing players would pay the winner whatever the difference was between their hand and the winning total.

Variations

Polignac

The classic French form of Jacks, dating back to the 17th century, and played by between four and six players. For four players cards between two and five are removed, for five or six players the black sevens are taken out too. The idea is to score as few points as possible, no points are awarded for tricks, one is given for tricks containing the jacks of hearts, diamonds and clubs, while the jack of spades – the 'polignac' – counts for two. If a player declares himself a 'general' at the start of a hand, it means he's intends to take all the tricks, if he does he deducts five points from his score, if not everybody else does and the jacks score as usual. Games finish after a prearranged number of hands and the scores are tallied.

King Albert

No. Players	One
Deck	Full
Aces	Low
Origin	USA
Simplicity factor	7
Skill factor	8
Suitability for children	7

A variation of Klondike that requires slightly more skill and is probably slightly more difficult to win.

All the cards are dealt out face-up in nine columns, with the one on the left having one card, and the far right one having nine. The seven cards left over are dealt into one face-up row at the foot of the layout.

The object is to build up the suits on the aces, once they are freed, but cards can only be moved singly, never as whole, pre-built sequences. However, unlike in Klondike, any card can be put into an empty column, thus with two empty columns sequences can be moved by 'bouncing' alternate cards between the two columns. Cards are put into play from the face-up row only when

no movement is possible on the layout. If all these
reserve cards have been used and play is blocked before

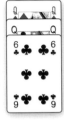

King Albert

the four suits have been collected on the aces, the game
is lost. If the suits have been collected it is won.

Klaberjass

No. Players	Two
Deck	No cards lower than seven
Score Sheet	Yes
Aces	High
Origin	Eastern Europe
Simplicity factor	4
Skill factor	9
Suitability for children	3
Suitability for gambling	6

An involved but fascinating game of Eastern European origin that became very popular in America. Sometimes this game is called Klob or Klobber.

Klaberjass is played by two players with a piquet pack (no cards lower than a seven). The aim is to take tricks and make melds. The cards' rankings are rearranged thus: in the non-trumps suits the 10 is moved to rank in between the ace and the king as the second highest valued card; as it is in the trumps suit, but with the jack and the nine, in that order, ranking above the ace. This means that the non-trumps suit runs A, 10, K, Q, J, 9, 8, 7 and trumps suit runs J, 9, A, 10, K, Q, 8, 7.

Klaberjass

The aim is to make melds

Six cards are dealt to each player – this can be done as two parcels of three. The next card is turned up to signify trumps, which the players then have the choice to accept or reject. The non-dealer goes first and can declare 'Accept' meaning he takes the suit as trumps; 'Pass' meaning the bid passes to the dealer or 'Schmeiss' meaning he would prefer that this hand was folded an the cards re-dealt. The dealer then has the chance to make the same bids. If both players pass, the bidding comes round to the non-dealer again who has the chance to 'make' trumps by naming any suit he wants. If he passes for a second time, the dealer has the chance to make trumps. If he, too, passes again, the hands are folded and the cards re-dealt. If both declare 'Schmeiss' then the hands are folded. If trumps have been accepted rather than made, a player who has the seven of that suit (the 'dix') may exchange it for the card that is turned up to signify trumps.

Both players will now proceed to make melds of running flushes within their hands. The non-dealer declares his highest value meld and the dealer attempts to match it. This is done in remarkably formal language. The non-dealer announces a meld by saying 'meld of 20 (or 50)'. The dealer replies 'Good', which means he can't match it and concedes; 'Not good' which means he can beat it or 'How high?' meaning he has the same and the players must compare top cards. In the event of a tied top card, if one suit is trumps it wins. If neither is then neither player scores. Whoever wins the declaration shows his opponent his winning meld and can score for any other he shows, the loser scores no points at all.

The idea, once play begins, is to win tricks with certain cards in them and score a prescribed schedule of points that are added to meld scores.

When the scores are counted up for each hand, if the player who accepted or made trumps scores less than his opponent, his score is given to his opponent and the first player scores nothing for the hand. If the player who didn't chose trumps scores lower, he keeps his score.

Scoring

- Three-card meld – 20
- Four-card meld – 50
- Jack of trumps ('jass') – 20
- Nine of trumps ('menel') – 14
- Any ace – 11
- Any ten – 10
- Any king – 4
- Any queen – 3
- Any jack other than of trumps – 2
- For taking the last trick – 10
- King and queen of trumps (a 'bella') – 20 bonus points (this can be made by either player if they hold and declare a 'bella')

Klondike

No. Players	One
Deck	Full
Score Sheet	No
Aces	Low
Origin	USA
Simplicity factor	8
Skill factor	7
Suitability for children	8

The most popular form of patience in the world, for many people in Europe and America Klondike is known as Patience or Solitaire, rather than by its true name.

A full deck is shuffled and seven cards are dealt in a row, with the first card (the one on the left) turned face-up. On top of these cards a second row of six is dealt, commencing with the first face-down card (second left) upon which a face-up card is dealt while the remaining five cards are covered with face-down cards. The next row is of five cards, following the same pattern. This continues until there is a triangular layout with the first column on the left being face-up card and the last one on the right being six face-

A Klondike starting line-up

Klondike

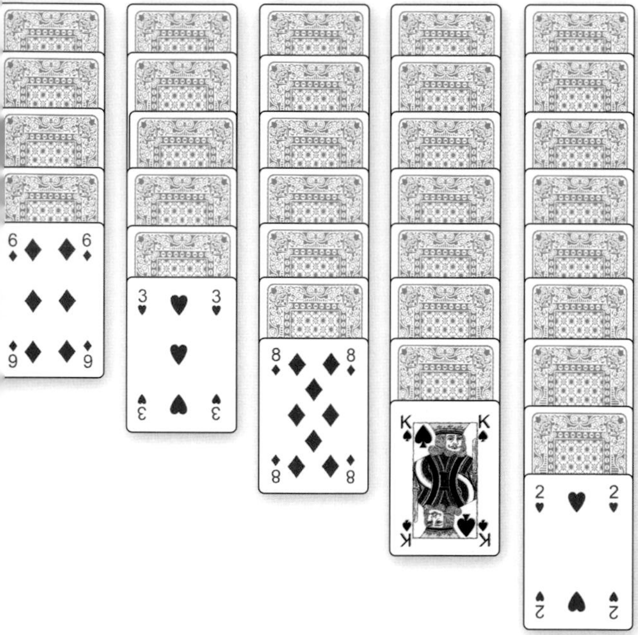

down cards with a face-up one at the bottom. The remaining cards are held in a face-down stack.

The object is to build up the suits in numerical order, starting from their respective aces. When the aces are face-up, uncovered or revealed through the deal of the pack, they are placed separately on the table. The twos of the same suit can then be placed on top of the aces and so on, so that four piles of cards, each a separate suit, are gradually built up.

In order to free up the face-down cards, the player builds descending numerical sequences of alternate red and black cards. As face-up cards are moved to put into a sequence or one of the suits being built, so the face-down card underneath it is turned over. Complete sequences can be moved to free up the face-down card beneath them, but only kings or sequences starting with a king can be moved into an empty column.

When no movement is possible, every third card in the stack is turned up and any of these can be put into play. If this still yields no movement, then the dealt-out stack is turned face-down, the top card put on the bottom and it is dealt out again in parcels of three. If three consecutive deals produce no movement, the game is lost. To win, every suit must be collected, in ascending sequence, on top of its respective ace.

Last In

No. Players	One
Deck	Full
Score Sheet	No
Aces	High
Simplicity factor	9
Skill factor	3
Suitability for children	10

An interesting variation of the standard trumps-n-trick-winning game, for between four and six players.

Using a full deck, six cards are dealt for four players, five for five players and four for six. The last card dealt – to the dealer – will be shown to the other players before the dealer takes it into his hand. The remaining cards are put into a stack.

Tricks are played for as normal, but before leading the next trick, the winner of each trick takes the top card from the stack and absorbs into his hand without making a discard. This means that some players will have more cards than others. As soon as all a player's cards are played he drops out, and the winner is the last man left in. If two players are left with one card each to contest a hand's final trick, the winner of the game is whichever one takes that trick.

Betting

Last In isn't really a gambler's game, so the best way to wager is for each player to put into a pot at the beginning of each hand and the winner takes all.

Monte Carlo

No. Players	One
Deck	Full
Score Sheet	No
Aces	High
Simplicity factor	9
Skill factor	3
Suitability for children	10

A quick and easy game of patience that relies greatly on how the cards are dealt.

A full pack is shuffled and 20 cards are dealt face-up in four rows of five, with the remainder held as a pot. If any cards are adjacent to one of similar face value, horizontally, vertically or diagonally, the pair is removed and put in a pile. (If three cards of the same value are next to each other, only two can be removed at one time.) Once all pairs from the layout have been removed, cards are dealt from the stack to replenish the layout by filling the holes. The object is to pair up all the cards and if the layout becomes such that no more pairing is possible, the game is lost.

My Ship Sails

No. Players . . . Four or more	
Deck . . . . . . One full deck for every six players	
Score Sheet . . . . No	
Simplicity factor 10	
Skill factor 6	
Suitability for children . . . 10	
Suitability for gambling . . . 0	

To get the maximum enjoyment out of this game, the trick is to play it quickly, so players have to make their minds up and make their moves within a very short time limit. When played like that, it's a fantastic game for children as it's easy to understand yet enjoys a high excitement factor.

Ideally, there should be half a dozen players, though it can be played with any number over three. If more than six are taking part, then two packs should be shuffled together.

A full deck is shuffled and seven cards are dealt to each player. The object is to collect seven cards in a single suit but of any denomination. To do this, the players

Someone's ship sails

select one discard from their hand and place it face-down on the table in front of them. Then everybody slides their discarded card to the player on the left and picks up the card that has been slid in front of them. This process is repeated until one player has all seven cards of the same suit, calls 'My ship sails' and wins the game. Often, the suit the winner finishes up with will not be the one he started out collecting, so it's not a good idea to be too inflexible.

Napoleon

No. Players	Two to six
Deck	Full
Score Sheet	No
Origin	England
Simplicity factor	9
Skill factor	7
Suitability for children	5
Suitability for gambling	9

In spite of the name, this is an English card game. It was very popular in the late 18th and early 19th centuries, and remains interesting thanks to its singular scoring system, which is based on what went on at the Battle of Waterloo.

Between two and six players are dealt five cards each from a full deck and bid as to how many tricks they think they can make, with the highest bid choosing trumps. Players can pass or bid 'Nullo' – to take no tricks. The game is then continued as for Whist, with the player who won the contract effectively playing against the rest. Once all the tricks have been played, the scores are added up.

A good hand for nullo

Scoring

If the contracted player makes his contract, he wins that number of points, unless the bid was for all five (a 'Napoleon') which wins five points and a bonus of five or it is a bid of nullo, which wins three points.

Betting

Napoleon is an ideal game for gambling, each player

should hold a stack of chips and a more involved scoring system can be applied, as follows. Successful contracts mean each player pays the winner that number of chips – including three for nullo. On a successful Napoleon, the winner is paid double by each player (10 chips) but only need pay each out singly if he loses. If the contract is for a Napoleon, the bidder has the chance to declare 'Wellington' which doubles the stakes to 20 for a win and a payout of 10 for a loss. Then there is a 'Blucher' which triples the bid to 30 for a win and 15 paid out for a loss. Wellingtons and Bluchers can be used if two players have bid Napoleons, with the higher winning the contract.

Oh Hell!

No. Players	Three or more
Deck	Full
Score Sheet	Yes
Origin	England
Simplicity factor	8
Skill factor	8
Suitability for children	8
Suitability for gambling	6

Sometimes, for obvious reasons, called Oh Well!, this is a pretty straightforward Whist-based game for upwards of three players that contains a couple of interesting twists.

In every deal the amount of cards dealt to each player goes up by one, so the first hand consists of one card, the second two, the third three, and so on, until it can't be raised, which signifies the end of the game. If there are three players there will be seventeen hands, four players thirteen hands, etc. After each deal, the first card of the remainder is turned over to signify trumps, but, in the case of, say, a four-player game where there will be no remainder on the final hand, it is played as No Trumps.

The fourth hand

Once the hands have been dealt, players bid for how many tricks they think they'll take – if it is none, as it may well be in the earlier rounds, they must declare 'Nullo'. Scores are kept cumulatively, and totalled up at the end of the game.

Scoring

At the end of each hand, the players that make their contract exactly score one point per trick and a ten-point bonus; players who go either over or under their contracted number of tricks score no points but do not incur any penalty. For making a contracted nullo, a player will score one point per trick in that hand, plus a ten-point bonus.

Betting

A cash-for-points system should be worked out before the game begins, with the losers paying the winner the differences between their hands and his.

Old Maid

No. Players	Three or more
Deck	Full
Score Sheet	No
Origin	France
Simplicity factor	10
Skill factor	4
Suitability for children	8

A classic children's card game, Old Maid originated several hundred years ago in France, where it was called Le Vieux Garçon (The Old Boy).

First one queen is removed from a full deck (in the French version it will be a jack) and all the remaining 51 cards are dealt out to the players. It doesn't matter if they aren't holding exactly the same number of cards each. The players look at their hands and sort them out into numerical pairs, which are put on the table in front of them. If a player holds three of a kind, a pair is put down but the remaining card is held on to. Four of a kind are put down as two pairs. The player to the left of the dealer then turns to the player on their left and offers their hand so the other

The Old Maid herself

player can take a card without seeing what it is. If this card makes a pair it is put down, if it doesn't it is absorbed into their hand. That player then turn to the player on his left and the process is repeated.

This continues until all the cards have been laid out in pairs and one player is left holding the odd queen. That player has lost and the others make the most of calling him or her an 'Old Maid'. (Or when playing in France, a 'Vieux Garçon'.)

Pinochle

No. Players............Two

Deck.........Two packs with everything below nines removed

Score Sheet.............Yes

Aces..................High

Origin...............Italian

Simplicity factor..........3

Skill factor...............8

Suitability for children....2

Suitability for gambling...8

Of Italian origin, Pinochle remains one of the most popular two-handed card games in America. Although it appears complicated, it is a game that seldom fails to repay the effort put into learning it. Scores are tallied for melds made and tricks taken that include certain scoring cards.

The game is played with two packs that have had everything lower than the nines removed, leaving 48 cards. The values are rearranged so that the ten ranks in between the ace and the king as the second highest card in each suit.

Each player is dealt 12 cards in lots of three, and the

Pinochle

Pinochle – ten points

next card is turned up to signify trumps. The players then play out a trick, which will be won in the usual manner, and the player who won it can put down a meld in front of him. Only one meld is played per turn, and cards used in melds can be used in future melds or played in tricks.

Before the next trick is played, each player will take up a card from the stockpile, and the game continues with each player having 12 cards in his hand (including the meld) until the stockpile is exhausted. After the stockpile is used up, no more melds will be made and the melds in front of each player are taken back into their hand. The last twelve tricks are then played out in the usual way.

Once all the tricks have been played, the tricks are turned face-up and scored for the honour cards contained in them. The winner of the last trick also scores ten bonus points.

The winner of a game of pinochle is the first player to 1000.

Scoring

- The melds are scored as follows:
- A, 10, K, Q, J of trumps – 150
- King and queen of trumps (a 'royal marriage') – 40
- King and queen of any other suit (a 'plain marriage' – 20
- Queen of spades and jack of diamonds ('pinochle') – 40

Pinochle

- Four aces (must all be of different suits) – 100
- Four kings (must all be of different suits) – 80
- Four queens (must all be of different suits) – 60
- Four jacks (must all be of different suits) – 40

If the card turned over for trumps is a nine (the 'dix') the dealer scores 10 points. If the dix was not revealed as the upturned card and a player has picked it up during the game, he can declare it and receive 10 bonus points.

In the tricks, aces score 11 points; tens score 10; kings – 4; queens – 3 and jacks – 2. Each trick score is rounded up to the next unit of 10 if it ends in a 7, an 8 or a 9; and it is rounded down to the previous 10 if it is below 7.

Piquet

No. Players	Two
Deck	Nothing lower than a seven
Score Sheet	Yes
Aces	High
Origin	England
Simplicity factor	2
Skill factor	8
Suitability for children	3
Suitability for gambling	7

A 500-year-old card game, Piquet may have a French name and French terminology, but it is in fact English. Charles I dedicated it to his French wife, hence the use of that language. Though it has been modernized a great deal over the years, Piquet enjoys a formal language and set of manners that serve to remind you that it was invented in a 15th-century palace.

Played by two players, it is this game's use of the abbreviated 32-card deck (nothing lower than a seven) that gave rise to the term 'piquet pack'. Each player is dealt twelve cards in six lots of two and the remaining

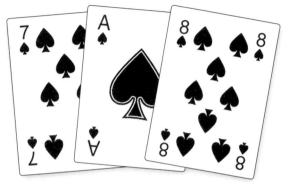

A flush

eight cards are placed face-down in one pile of three and one of five. Now the game (called a 'partie') can begin and the idea is to win points by making melds and winning tricks. The process by which this is done is in four discernible stages.

1) The Discard

The dealer discards up to five cards, replacing them from

the stockpile of five, and then looks at any of the five he decides not to take up, without showing them to his opponent. The non-dealer then discards up to any of the number left in both stockpiles combined, and look at any of the cards he doesn't take up.

2) Making Combinations

The players arrange their hands into combinations of flushes, numerically sequential flushes and numerical groupings, which will be matched against the opponent's respective groupings. Cards from their hands can be used in more than one combination. At this point, they will decide which of their combinations they will 'declare', which means to match against their opponent's.

3) Declaring Combinations

In classic piquet this is done with a formality that verges on the tedious, and although the process is explained below, it is rarely adhered to:

Piquet

The non-dealer will first announce his longest flush (or 'point') by saying 'A point of ...'. If the dealer can't match it he replies 'Good' and concedes the points. If he can beat it he replies 'Not good' and takes the points himself. If he can match it he asks 'How many?' and the non-dealer replies 'A point of ..., I score ...' and states the numerical value of his point. The dealer responds either with 'Good' meaning he can't beat it; 'Not good' meaning he can or 'Equal' if his is the same value. If this happens the points are abandoned.

At the end of each point declaration, the winner has to declare his winning point and the score he got for it: 'A point of ..., I score ...'

Next the non-dealer will declare his longest running flush, or 'sequence' as it is called. To declare a sequence, the conversation is essentially the same except the announcement made would be 'A sequence of ...'. In the event of a tie the dealer will say 'how high?', which precipitates the announcement of the highest card.

Finally the non-dealer declares his best meld, with

the declaration 'A trio of ...' or 'A quatorze of ...'. Of course, melds cannot tie.

4) The Play

After the declarations have finished, the tricks are played for, in the usual manner but without a trump suit.

Scores are totalled after each hand, and the winner is the player with the highest number of points after the prescribed number of hands, or the first to reach 'rubicon' or 100 points.

Scoring

It is possible for either player to score 10 points in between the deal and the discard if they announce a 'carte blanche' – a hand featuring no court cards.

When the two players match their best 'points', the one with the longest will score one point for each card in it. If two 'points' contain the same number of cards, the numerical value is totalled, with court cards counting as 10, aces as 11 and the point with the highest value wins.

Piquet

Again, one point is awarded for each card. Players can only score for the one flush they decide to declare, even if they have others in their hand.

Whoever holds the longest sequence, in any suit, wins and a player can score for every sequence in his hand. If the sequences are the same length, then the one with the highest top card wins – if that is the same then there is no score awarded. The scores for sequences are:

- Three cards ('tierce') – 3
- Four cards ('quart') – 4
- Five cards ('quint') –15
- Six cards ('sixième') – 16
- Seven cards ('septième') – 17
- Eight cards ('huitième') – 18

Three of a kind or four of a kind, providing it's aces, kings, queens, jacks or tens, score three points (a 'trio') and four points (a 'quatorze') respectively, for each such meld the holder of the highest has in his hand. If there is a tie, the remaining grouping of the cards of the highest numerical order is the winner.

Players score one point for each trick won and one extra point for taking the last trick.

Other bonus scores are as follows:

- For taking seven tricks – 10
- For taking all the tricks ('capot') – 40
- For the non-dealer scoring 30 points before the dealer scores ('pique') – 30
- For scoring 30 points before play begins ('repique') – 60

Scores are kept cumulatively on a score sheet.

Betting

The difference between the winner's and the loser's scores can be translated into a cash value at a pre-arranged rate.

Pisha Pasha

No. Players	Two
Deck	Full
Score Sheet	No
Aces	High
Origin	Eastern Europe
Simplicity factor	10
Suitability for children	8

One step up from Snap!, this is a quick, easy and fun two-handed game for very young children.

A full deck of cards is dealt into two face-down piles, with one being placed in front of each player. The players simultaneously turn cards over to form separate face-up piles in front of each of them. When both players turn up cards of the same suit, they call 'Pisha Pasha' and the whichever has played the card of the higher numerical value takes both upturned piles and puts them on the bottom of their face-down stash. The winner is the first player to capture all the cards, but if their stash runs out while the other player still has cards, the face-up pile will be turned over and used to continue the game.

Poker

No. Players	Ideally no more than seven
Deck	Full (usually)
Score Sheet	No
Aces	High
Simplicity factor	2
Skill factor	10
Suitability for children	2
Suitability for gambling	10

The basic rules of poker are actually pretty straightforward but, like Bridge, there are so many subtleties involved in the playing and betting that literally hundreds of books have been written on the subject. What follows here is how to play, score and bet in the most basic way. After that, it's up to you how far you want to progress in the game. There is also a myriad of different variations of poker, and listed below are a few of the more commonplace examples.

Usually played with between three and seven players, always with a full deck, the idea is to finish up with the highest-rated combination possible from a five-

Poker

A royal flush

card hand. The rankings of the various hands are as follows, and they never change whatever version of the game is being played. The hands are, in descending order:

• Royal flush – ace, king, queen, jack and 10 of the same suit.

• Straight flush – five cards of the same suit in numerical order.

• Four of a kind – four cards of the same numerical value, the highest being four aces.

- Full house – two of one numerical value, three of another, determined by the value of the trio.
- Flush – five of the same suit but not in numerical order, determined by the highest card or, in the event of a tie, the second highest.
- Straight – five cards of numerical sequence but not in the same suit, determined by the highest card.
- Three of a kind – three of the same value, determined by which is numerically higher.
- Two pairs – two different pairs, determined by the highest pair in each hand or, in the event of a tie, the second pair.
- A pair – determined by which is higher or, in the event of a tie, by the highest card in the hand outside the pair.
- High card – if none of the above are held, the winner is determined by whoever has the highest card, or, in a tie, the second highest.

When twos are wild – which will be decided on at the start of a game – the highest hand is five of a kind, which is four of a kind and a two. If a wild two is used against a 'natural hand' – one that has made the same combination without recourse to a two – the natural takes preference.

Betting

Each player will 'ante up', that is, put in a specified amount in order to be part of the hand about to be dealt. Then the betting goes round the table from the left of the dealer. The first player to bet will 'open', by putting in any amount he fancies (providing it doesn't exceed the agreed limit), or 'fold' (sometimes known as 'drop') and throw his cards in to take no further part in that hand. If the first player opened, the next player can 'raise', which is to put a greater amount than the first player, or 'call', that is put in the same amount, or fold. The same options are open to the next player, who, if the previous player raised, has to match or go above that amount, or else fold. Once all remaining players have merely called and there are no more raises, the hands are compared with the winner taking the pot.

Variations

The more common forms of poker are:

Straight Poker

Players are singly dealt a hand of five cards each, and play that through the rounds of betting, with no chance to change any of them. Once everybody has finished betting, the hands are compared and the highest takes the pot.

Draw Poker

Players are singly dealt a hand of five cards each, and a round of betting takes place in which players can drop out. Once that is finished, starting on the dealer's left and moving round the table, each player has the opportunity to discard as many cards as they want and 'draw' (get dealt) fresh ones form the deck. Then another round of betting takes place, in which players are again free to drop out. Once that is over, the remaining players compare hands.

Five-Card Stud

Very popular in America, this is the game that the most daring poker players go for. It involves more nerve and judgement than draw poker as everybody can see four of the cards in every player's hands.

Each player is dealt a card face-down and then a card face-up. They inspect their face-down card and leave it hidden, then the player with the highest face-up card opens the betting, or folds his hand. After that round of betting every player left in is dealt another face-up card and the player with the highest scoring cards showing opens the next round of betting. The same process is repeated twice more until every player still in the game has four face-up cards and one, his 'hole card', face-down. The betting now goes round the table once more before the players reveal their hole cards to make their hands.

Stripped Deck Poker

This is Draw or Five-Card Stud where there are only

A full house, fours over kings

three or four players and the low cards – twos to fives –
are removed from the pack. This obviously increases the
chances of getting high-scoring hands.

Wild Card Poker

Exactly what it says, this is any game of poker in which
it has been agreed beforehand that one denomination of
card – usually the deuces – can count as any other card.

Pontoon

No. Players	Any
Deck	Full
Score Sheet	No
Aces	High and low
Origin	Europe
Simplicity factor	6
Skill factor	8
Suitability for children	7
Suitability for gambling	10

What follows is the domestic version of the casino game often called Blackjack (in the USA) or Twenty-one. It can be played by any number of players, each of whom is individually playing against the bank, i.e. the dealer.

The idea of the game is to get a hand that adds up to 21, or as close to it as possible, preferably in just two cards.

The dealer deals each player one card, face-down. Players look at their card and put down a bet depending on its value. Once betting is complete, the banker looks at his card and, if he chooses, can ask the players, en masse, to double their wagers. Any who don't wish to must drop out and lose their stake.

The classic pontoon

Each player, and the bank, is then dealt a second card. Any player with a 'pontoon' – an ace and a picture card or a ten – turns his cards face-up to declare it. If there are no pontoons among the players' hands, the players will, in turn, start playing against the bank by announcing they will 'twist' or 'stick'. If a player twists, the dealer deals him a face-up card and the player takes it into his hand. If that hand is still sufficiently short of 21 to warrant another card, they will twist again. Once they are satisfied with the total, they say they will stick, and the dealer moves on to the next player to repeat the process. If a player's total exceeds 21, they are 'bust', must fold their hand and the dealer takes their stake.

After all the players have finished, the dealer turns over his cards and plays his hand in the same way. If the dealer has a pontoon, he beats every other hand – even other pontoons, as in the event of a tie the dealer has the advantage – and takes in all the stake money. If he doesn't and another player does, he pays that player the value of his stake and then commences to play against the rest. If any player has twisted three times and remains below 21 it is a 'five-card trick' and the actual value only counts if the dealer has a five-card trick too, then the lowest total wins. Otherwise, players that have totals closer to 21 than the dealer achieves get paid their stake, those that don't lose.

Players who are dealt two cards the same in the original deal have the option to 'split' – they are dealt one more card to each of those held, and play each as a separate hand against the dealer, repeating the original stake. When a player makes pontoon, providing the dealer doesn't, he takes over the deal from the next hand.

Scoring

Aces can count as 11 or as one, depending on what works best for the player; picture cards are ten; everything else is at face value. A pontoon beats everything, a five-card trick is second best and after that it's whichever totals are nearest to 21 without going bust.

Red Dog

No. Players	Three or more
Score Sheet	No
Deck	Full
Score Sheet	No
Aces	High
Origin	USA
Simplicity factor	8
Skill factor	9
Suitability for children	0
Suitability for gambling	10

A fast-moving, rather exciting gambling game that belies its apparent simplicity as the stakes involved can quickly mount up.

Each player puts a specified amount into the pot, then each is dealt five cards from a full deck, with the remainder put face-down in the centre of the table. In turn, from the dealer's left, each player bets that they can beat the top card of the pack (which has yet to be turned over) with a card from their hand. The minimum bet is one unit and the maximum is the entire pot. The card is then revealed and the players have to beat it by showing a higher card in the same suit. If they can, they show the

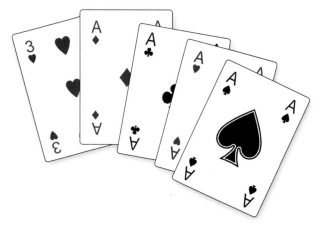

The perfect Red Dog hand

winning card only and take the amount wagered from the pot; if not their stake goes into the pot and they don't show their cards. As the value of the pot can change during a round of play, a player who bets 'the pot' wins or loses the amount that is in it at the end of that round. If more than one player bets 'the pot' and is successful in the same round, they share between them, equally, whatever is in the pot at the end of that round.

After a round has been played, the turned-up card is put face-down on the bottom of the pack, as are the players' thrown in hands, and the deal is passed to the left. Whatever is in the pot from game to game is left there, which means it can build up to quite a sum if a few unsuccessful big bets are made. If it is won, then the players contribute again to a new one.

Variations

Three-Card Red Dog

This is the version of the game usually played in casinos. It is not possible to hold one card in every suit and the 'perfect Red Dog hand' of four aces cannot be held by any player.

Rolling Stone

No. Players ..... Four to six
Deck ......Varies according to the number of players
Score Sheet ... If not playing for money
Aces .... High
Origin .... France
Simplicity factor......... 10
Skill factor 6
Suitability for children.... 7
Suitability for gambling... 8

This game originated in northern Europe and was called Enfle. It is a quick-paced trick-winning game for between four and six players that is ideal for wagering small amounts.

If being played with four players, all cards below the seven are removed from the deck, if there are five players the sixes and fives are included, if six players then only the twos are removed. Each player is dealt eight cards, there are no trumps and players must follow suit when playing a trick. If any player can't he takes up the other cards that would have made up the trick and incorporates them into his hand. If more than one player can't follow suit the last one in the sequence to play takes up the cards. If everybody follows suit then the trick is gathered up and put aside, to play no further part in proceedings.

The winner is the first player to get rid of all his cards, and he collects one pre-agreed unit from each other player for each card they are left holding. Another unconventional feature of this game is that as soon as a player has played his last card, the game stops, even if it is in the middle of a trick and the cards, quite literally held are the cards to be counted. If not gambling, then the losing players will score a point for each card they are left holding, and after a prearranged time or number of games, the winner will be the one with the least points.

Royal Marriage

No. Players	One
Deck	Full
Score Sheet	No
Origin	England
Simplicity factor	9
Skill factor	3
Suitability for children	8

Often called Betrothal, the aim of this romantically inclined patience game is to unite a king and queen that have been set apart from each other.

To start a king and queen of the same suit are removed from a full pack while it is being shuffled and cut, and are placed one each on the top and bottom of the pack, (it doesn't matter which of the cards goes where). The cards are dealt out across the table in a face-up line. Every time a card appears with cards of the same suit as each other on either side – for example, ten of hearts, four of clubs, three of hearts – the card in the middle (in this case the four of clubs) is removed. The gap closed up and the deal continues.

A royal marriage

The object is to remove all the cards so that the selected royal couple end up next to each other on the table. If all the cards are dealt out and it is not possible to remove any, the game is lost.

Rummy

No. Players......Two to six	
Deck....................Full	
Score Sheet............Yes	
Aces..................High	
Origin.................USA	
Simplicity factor..........4	
Skill factor...............8	
Suitability for children....6	
Suitability for gambling...4	

So named as the game began its life as Rum Poker in the Wild West, Rummy and its variations remain among the most popular card games in the world.

If two players are playing they are dealt 10 cards each; for three or four players, seven cards; for five or six, six cards. Undealt cards are placed in a face-down stack on the table, with the top of this stack turned face-up and placed next to it.

The players' aim is to 'meld' their hands into sets of three or four of a kind, or sequences of four cards or more in the same suit. They do this by, in turn, exchanging single cards in their hands for cards on the

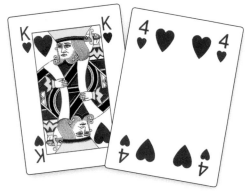

The King wins

table. Players can take either the top card of the face-down stack or the upturned card. They then discard any card from their hand onto the face-up pile. Unless a player is going for 'rummy' – all the cards in their hand in sequence – once melds are made they are placed face-up in front of the player who made them and all players are free to add cards to each other's melds at any time during the game. The winner is the first player to get rid of all their cards either by calling 'rummy' or by placing them on theirs or other players' melds.

Scoring

Once a player has dropped out, the denominations of each other player's hand is totalled (picture cards count as 10, aces as one). If the winning player has made rummy, the totals of every other hand in that particular round are doubled. The overall winner is the player with the least number of points to their name at the end of the prescribed time.

Betting

A cash-for-points system is the best way to approach this, and if there are more than two players, it would help if one of them was a mathematician.

Variations

Gin Rummy

A version for two players, who are dealt 10 cards each and aim to go 'Gin' by arranging all of those cards in one sequence. No early melds are allowed.

Knock Rummy

A version of Gin Rummy that is ended early if a player knocks the table after he has picked up a card but before he discards. Both players then meld as many cards as possible (there is no adding to the opponent's melds) and add up the scores of their remainders. If the knocker is lower, he scores the difference plus 10; if the knocker is beaten, the knockee scores the difference plus 25.

Boathouse Rummy

Here if players take from the face-up pile they must take from the face-down pile too, yet only discard one card. There are no melds in this version and to win a player must go rummy with the entire hand.

Rummy

Michigan Rummy

This version sees the face-up pile spread out so a player can take a card that was discarded a while ago, provided they take all the cards on top of it. This card must then immediately be put down in a meld or added to an existing one. Scoring is back to front here, with players earning points for the melds they put down, and the winner of each hand gaining the points from the cards the other players are left holding. Aces can be high or low and count as 15 points for those left in opponents' hands or as one point if at the end of a low end meld (four, three, two, ace).

Continental Rummy

Here two packs of cards are shuffled together. Each player is dealt 15 cards (this can be done in threes). Three- or four-of-a-kind melds are not permitted and cards must be arranged in numerical sequences of three or more. No melds are laid down early, and to win players must meld their entire hand into one of the following combinations: five melds of three cards; three of four cards and one of three or one five, a four and two threes. Jokers are wild, aces can be high or low and scoring is the same as in regular Rummy.

S

S

S

Scotch Whist

No. Players..	Three to seven
Deck ..	Nothing below a six
Score Sheet............	Yes
Aces	High
Origin	Not Scotland!
Simplicity factor..........	8
Skill factor	8
Suitability for children	7
Suitability for gambling ...	6

This isn't really Whist as the tricks taken don't count for anything, and it's probably safe to assume that it isn't from Scotland either. But it is a fun, fast-moving game in which the idea is to capture certain cards.

Although it can be played by different numbers, the classic form has two teams of two seated opposite each other, with a pack that has every card below the six removed. In the trumps suit the highest ranked card is the jack. Each player is dealt nine cards, with the final one being turned up as trumps then taken into the dealer's hand. The number of tricks taken by each pair isn't important, it's what's in the tricks that count. The winners are the pair who gets to 41 points first.

Jacks high

Scoring

Teams score the following points for finishing up with certain trump cards: the jack – 11 points; the ace – 4, the king – 3; the queen – 2; the ten –10. They also score one point for each card over ten (half the pack) they finish up with.

Variations

When played with six people (when, confusingly, it is sometimes called French Whist) they are in three teams of two, but if it involves three, five or seven players, they all play individually. With three players they have 12 cards each; with five they have seven; and seven they have five cards. Odd cards can be used to signify trumps but are of no other use, and points scored for counting cards are awarded one for every card a player finishes up with over the number he started with.

Slap Jack

No. Player	Three or more
Deck	Full
Score Sheet	No
Aces	High
Simplicity factor	10
Skill factor	4
Suitability for children	10

A good game for very young children as it's one of the more physical card games.

A pack of cards is dealt out face-down into piles in front of each player. If there are many players, more than one pack can be used. In quick succession, each player turns his top card over to form a pile in the centre of the table. As soon as a jack is turned over, every player has to slap a hand down on top of the pile of upturned cards. The player whose hand is actually on the pile – the first to slap the jack – takes the pile and puts it face-down beneath his own.

This continues until one player has all the cards and wins the game – as players lose all their cards, they drop out.

Snap!

No. Players	More than two
Deck	ull
Simplicity factor	10
Skill factor	2
Suitability for children	9

The ultimate children's card game and probably everybody's first experience of playing cards. It hasn't changed at all over the years, or should that be centuries?

A full deck of cards is dealt out face-down in piles in front of each player – more than one deck can be shuffled together if there are many players. In rotation to the left, players turn over their top card on to pile in the centre. When two cards of the same value are turned up simultaneously, the players all shout 'Snap!'. The first one to do so collects the pile in the centre, turns it upside down and puts it on the bottom of their own pile. The winner is the one to collect all the cards.

A slight variation is for the players to each make their own piles of upturned cards, again turning them

Snap!

over in rotation. When the cards on two piles match and 'Snap!' is called, the winner wins those two piles only.

Snap!

Snip Snap Snorem

No. Players	Three to eight
Deck	Full
Score Sheet	No
Origin	England
Simplicity factor	8
Skill factor	6
Suitability for children	10
Suitability for gambling	7

If played at speed, this fairly rowdy stopping game is one that younger children are guaranteed to enjoy.

All the cards in a full deck are dealt out to the players, who can number between three and eight. If any cards are left over, the top one is turned over as a starter, if not then the player on the dealer's left starts by playing any card from his hand. The next player round to have a card of the same numerical value plays it on top and says 'Snip', the next player with a card of that value plays it on top and declares 'Snap' and the player with the final card of that denomination plays it to call 'Snorem'. Any players who haven't got a card of that value miss a turn, and the player who called

Snip Snap Snorem

'Snip!'... 'Snap!'... 'Snorem!'

'Snorem' starts things off again with a card of any denomination he chooses.

The winner is the first player to get rid of all his cards. As players can look at their hands there are more tactics involved in this game than you might at first think!

Betting

Chips can be paid to the winner by the losers at the rate of one per card held when the game stops.

Variations

Jig

Instead of playing cards of the same numerical value, cards are played in same suit sequence, up or down, so the seven of spades would be followed by either the eight or the six. The sequence would then continue in that direction for four cards only until the player who called 'Snorem' starts another sequence.

Earl of Coventry

The same as Snip Snap Snorem except the lead player, if he played a four, would call 'That's as good as four can be'. The next player to play a four would say 'There's a four as good as he'. The third continues with 'There's the best of all the three', while the fourth player would finish the rhyme off with 'And there's the Earl of Coventry!'

Stealing The Old Man's Bundle

No. Players	Three to four
Deck	Full
Score Sheet	No
Simplicity factor	6
Skill factor	7
Suitability for children	10

An entertaining children's game, for between two and four players, that requires a little more thought than most.

Each player is singly dealt four cards and four cards are put face-up in the middle of the table. Going in rotation to the left from the dealer, if a player can numerically – or picture for picture – match any card in the centre with one in his hand, he takes the card from the centre and puts it face-up with his own card near him on the table. It is his 'bundle'. If he can match more than one with the same card he will take them all into his bundle, or, if a card in his hand matches the top card on another player's bundle, when it is his turn he can take that whole bundle. If he had no matches in his hand he must put a card from his hand face-up in the row in the centre, which is called 'trailing'.

After all players have played all their cards, each is dealt another four, with no more being put into the centre. When all the cards are played out, the winner is the one with the most cards in front of them, in other words, the biggest bundle.

Trefoil

No. Players	One
Deck	Full
Aces	Low
Origin	France
Simplicity factor	8
Skill factor	3
Suitability for children	6

A deceptively tricky game of patience that, on first approach, appears very easy but is really rather difficult to win.

All four aces are removed from a full deck, and placed face-up on the table as bases for building up their respective suits. The remainder of the cards are then shuffled and dealt into sixteen face-up piles of three, which are fanned out to resemble the 'trefoils' or three-leafed clovers of the title. The idea is to build up the suits from two upward with top cards from any of the trefoils. However, to free up cards locked inside trefoils, top cards can be moved on to other trefoil top cards – provided they are of the same suit and numerically descending – to create descending builds.

Whole builds can also be transferred in this way.

If all moves are 'blocked' – no cards can be placed on descending builds or the suits – trefoils without builds on them are gathered up, shuffled and re-dealt, once again as threes, with any left over making the final trefoil of one or two cards. Three such re-deals are allowed, and if a game gets blocked after that, it is lost.

Variations

Midnight Oil

Here the aces are dealt out as part of the trefoils and have to be freed up like any other card in order to serve as bases.

House in the Woods

Midnight Oil played with two packs shuffled together and the eight aces dealt into the trefoils.

Card Games

Trefoil

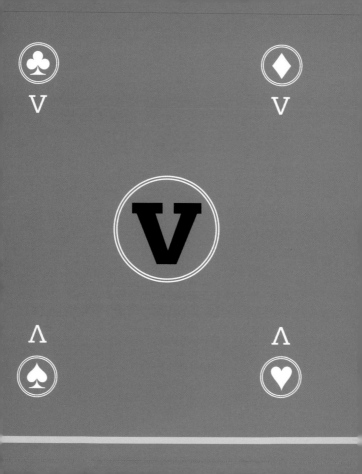

Vint

No. Players	Four
Deck	Full
Score Sheet	Yes
Aces	High
Origin	Russia
Simplicity factor . . .	Game 8
	Scoring 5
Skill factor	Game 5
	Scoring 5
Suitability for children 2
Suitability for gambling . . . 6

A derivative of Whist which has a few similarities to Bridge, especially in the scoring and bidding processes, Vint originated in Tsarist Russia. The game is played by two teams of two seated opposite each other.

A full deck is dealt out, leaving each player with 13 cards. Once they have inspected their hands, the bidding begins for how many more tricks than 'book' (six tricks) they think they can make, nominating their preferred suit as trumps. The highest numerate bid would be 'seven', and the suits are, in descending order – no trumps, hearts, diamonds, clubs, spades. 'Seven, no trumps' is therefore the highest possible bid.

Unlike in Bridge, there is no dummy in Vint, so both players of the partnership play out the hands as in any Whist-based game. The player who made the successful contract bid leads and once the hand is finished, scoring is very similar to Bridge with a horizontal line drawn across the score sheet and different scores entered 'above the line' and 'below the line'.

Scoring

The partnerships score for the tricks either partner makes. The scores entered below the line are called 'game points' and are awarded to each partnership for tricks made during each hand. The amount depends on the value of the contract and are 10 points per trick for a bid of one; 20 points for a bid of two; and so on up to 70 points per trick for a bid of seven. As soon as a partnership reaches 500 below-the-line points the game ends.

Vint

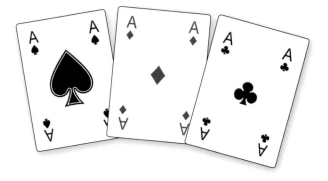

Bonus points are entered above the line and are :
- For winning a game – 1000
- For winning a rubber (two out of three games) – 2000
- For taking 12 tricks in a game (a little slam) – 1000
- For taking a little slam if 'six' was bid – 6000
- For taking 13 tricks in a game (a grand slam) – 2000
- For taking a grand slam if 'seven' was bid – 12000

Also entered above the line are the following honour points:

Honour cards are the ace, king, queen, jack and ten

of trumps and whichever pair has the most of them in the tricks they have won scores ten times the tricks' value for each. If it was a no trumps hand, whichever pair holds the most aces scores 25 times the tricks' value for each – if both partnerships hold two aces in a no trumps round there is no score. The losers' honour cards are not counted.

If any single player holds three aces or a single-suit three-card numerical sequence he scores 500 points for the partnership – either is called a 'coronet'. If he has the fourth ace he racks up another 500; as does every other card over three in the sequence. If the sequence is in trumps, the scores are doubled to 1000 and it is called a 'double coronet'.

After one pair has won two games by scoring 500 below the line points twice, the winners of the 'rubber' are decided by counting each partnerships' total of above- and below-the-line points.

Betting

A pre-agreed cash value for points system is the best way, with amounts paid on the difference between the winning and losing totals.

Variations

Preference

A less involved version of Vint, for three players, Preference uses a piquet pack, with no trumps and is much more suitable for gambling. Each player puts a pre-agreed amount in the pot and the deal gives them ten cards each with the remaining two being put aside as the 'widow'. Bidding then begins for how many tricks each player believes they could make over 'book' – in this case five – with their own choice of trumps. The hierarchy of the suits is the same as above. The contract winner effectively plays against the other two, and if he makes the contract he takes money from the pot depending on the value of the contract, for a prearranged amount. If he fails to make it he puts money into the put at the same value.

W

W

War

No. Players . . . Two or more	
Deck . . . . Full	
Score Sheet . . . . No	
Simplicity factor 10	
Skill factor 0	
Suitability for children 8	

An exciting kids' game for two or more players (here the two-handed version is explained). War is sometimes called Everlasting due to the length of time a game can take, it is ideal for long journeys or rainy holidays.

A full deck is dealt out into two face-down piles, one in front of each player. They each turn their top card over on to the table side by side. Whoever plays the numerically highest card, regardless of suit, wins both cards and puts them, face-down, on the bottom of their pile. Should they both be of equal value, the players must 'go to war', which means they each play a card face-down next to their original tied card, they then play another card face-up on top of it and the highest card takes all six. If those cards tie also, then the war goes on

Going to war

– another card is played face-down before the next one is played face-up. This will continue until there is a winner from the face-up cards and that player takes all the cards in the centre, which are sorted to face-down and put on the bottom of his pile.

The game continues until one player wins by taking all the cards. Or one of the players dies of old age!

Variations

The game can be played with more players and more than one deck, but cards left over from the deal should be removed so that all the hands are equal. It is played exactly as before, with the winner taking all the cards in the centre, and when the winning cards are part of a tie, then all the players join in the war that is again played out until somebody wins it. Once a player loses all of his cards, he drops out and the rest carry on until there is a clear winner.

Whist

No. Players	Two to four
Deck	Full
Score sheet	Yes
Aces	High
Origin	England
Simplicity factor	8
Skill factor	7
Suitability for children	7
Suitability for gambling	6

First described by Edmund Hoyle in his 18th-century book of cards games, this straightforward trumps 'n' tricks game is the foundation for many other games.

In its most basic form, Whist is played with a full deck by four players in pairs, sitting opposite each other. Each is singly dealt 13 cards and the last card is turned up to signify trumps, then taken into the dealer's hand. Tricks are then played for in the conventional manner, with players following the suit led or if they can't, discarding or trumping and the winners are the partnership who have won the most tricks. The deal rotates to the left after each hand and scoring is

Diamonds, as trumps, wins the trick

optional. In this version, each pair scores one point for each trick they make over 'book' (six tricks) and the winners are the first to seven points. There are, however, several variations that can make the game much more interesting.

Betting

A cash-for-points system can be worked out.

Variations

English Whist

This is played the same way, but scored far more formally. Each trick over book scores one point each; winning a game scores five points; and within the taken tricks, the team holding most of the honour cards – ace, king, queen and jack of trumps – win bonus points, four points for four honours, two for three. If a team wins a game by five points to nil it wins a 'treble', or three extra points; if it wins by five to one, it scores a 'double', or two extra points; while a win of five to three or four is a 'single', earning one extra point. The first team to win two games wins the rubber and two bonus points.

German Whist

This version is played with two players, who start with 13 cards each from a full deck and the next one is turned up for trumps. Once the first trick is won (they are played for as in basic Whist) the winner picks up the turned up card and the loser takes the face-down one beneath it and the next card is turned up. The winner of the previous trick leads and the procedure with the pack is repeated until the pack is exhausted. The remaining tricks are then played out and the winner is the one with the most tricks. This version is ideal for gambling, as the loser can pay the winner a pre-agreed sum for each trick his total is short of his opponent's.

Bid Whist

Bid Whist is played by two teams of two, but the trumps are bid for as players nominate the number of tricks they think they can make plus the number of honour cards they believe they can finish up with. One point is awarded for each trick and the honour cards are scored as one point for each. Scores are cumulative, and if the successful bidder makes the contract, they score the difference between their total and their opponents', while if they fail to make contract, they score nothing and the other side gets their full score.

Knockout Whist

This can be played by up to seven players, and seven cards are dealt to each with the next card turned up to signify trumps. It is played as the basic game, except any player who doesn't make a single trick in a hand is 'knocked out' to take no further part in the game and the winner is the last player left in. The game could be won in the first hand if a player takes all seven tricks.

GLOSSARY

Aces High: The ace is the highest ranked card in each suit.

Aces Low: The ace is the lowest ranked card in each suit.

Bid: To declare how many tricks a player thinks they will make from that hand.

Carte Blanche: A hand with no picture cards in it.

Cut: Divide the pack in half and place the bottom half on top of the top half. This happens after shuffling but before dealing.

Court Cards: Jack, Queen and King of any suit (see also Face Cards and Picture Cards).

Deal: Distribute the correct number of cards among the players, methods will vary.

Deuce: A two of any suit.

Discards: Cards that players have considered and rejected.

Face Cards: Jack, Queen and King of any suit (see also

Court Cards and Picture Cards).

Follow Suit: Play a card of the same suit as the last one played.

Hand: The cards a player holds, or play that results from any one deal.

Knock: To be unable to follow suit and signify thus by knocking the table.

Lead: The first player round the table plays a card and establishes the suit for that hand.

Meld: A group of cards of the same rank or in sequence – usually three cards, but the number varies from game to game.

Misdeal: When the cards are dealt out incorrectly, in which case they will be gathered in, shuffled and redealt.

Pass: To miss your turn when it comes to bidding or playing.

Picture Cards: Jack, Queen and King of any suit (see also Court Card and Face Card).

Piquet Pack: A 32-card pack from which all spot cards

lower than the sevens have been removed.

Pot: The amount bet on a hand, collected in the middle of the table or the stack of cards left over from the deal and placed face down on the table to be drawn from.

Rank: A card's numerical or pictorial value, or the order in which these rankings occur.

Revoke: Not following suit.

Slam: A single player or partnership wins all the tricks in one hand.

Spot Cards: Any card, of any suit, ranked from two to ten.

Suit: Hearts, Clubs, Diamonds and Spades are the four suits.

Trey: A three of any suit.

Trick: The cards collected when each player has played a card in accordance of the rules of whatever game is being played.

Trump: A predecided suit that will take preference over all other suits – any trump card will beat any card from any other suit.

Upcard: The card that is turned face up at the end of a deal to designate trumps.

Wild card: Can be nominated as a card of any value.